The Role of Advisory Committees in Biomedical Education and Workforce Development:

Emerging Research and Opportunities

Argentina Ornelas
University of Texas MD Anderson Cancer Center, USA

Julie Neal
Independent Researcher, USA

A volume in the Advances in Educational Marketing, Administration, and Leadership (AEMAL) Book Series

IGI Global
DISSEMINATOR OF KNOWLEDGE

Published in the United States of America by
IGI Global
Information Science Reference (an imprint of IGI Global)
701 E. Chocolate Avenue
Hershey PA, USA 17033
Tel: 717-533-8845
Fax: 717-533-8661
E-mail: cust@igi-global.com
Web site: http://www.igi-global.com

Library of Congress Cataloging-in-Publication Data

Names: Ornelas, Argentina, 1981- author.
Title: The role of advisory committees in biomedical education and workforce development : emerging research and opportunities / by Argentina Ornelas and Julie Neal.
Description: Hershey, PA : Information Science Reference, [2018] | Includes bibliographical references and index.
Identifiers: LCCN 2017028584| ISBN 9781522540830 (h/c) | ISBN 9781522540847 (ebook)
Subjects: LCSH: Medical education--Research--United States. | Medical personnel--Training of--United States. | Advisory boards--Medicine.
Classification: LCC R745 .O76 2018 | DDC 610.71--dc23 LC record available at https://lccn.loc.gov/2017028584

This book is published in the IGI Global book series Advances in Educational Marketing, Administration, and Leadership (AEMAL) (ISSN: 2326-9022; eISSN: 2326-9030)

British Cataloguing in Publication Data
A Cataloguing in Publication record for this book is available from the British Library.

Advances in Educational Marketing, Administration, and Leadership (AEMAL) Book Series

ISSN:2326-9022
EISSN:2326-9030

Editor-in-Chief: Siran Mukerji, IGNOU, India, Purnendu Tripathi, IGNOU, India

MISSION

With more educational institutions entering into public, higher, and professional education, the educational environment has grown increasingly competitive. With this increase in competitiveness has come the need for a greater focus on leadership within the institutions, on administrative handling of educational matters, and on the marketing of the services offered.

The **Advances in Educational Marketing, Administration, & Leadership (AEMAL) Book Series** strives to provide publications that address all these areas and present trending, current research to assist professionals, administrators, and others involved in the education sector in making their decisions.

COVERAGE

- Academic Pricing
- Governance in P-12 and Higher Education
- Technologies and Educational Marketing
- Educational Management
- Educational Finance
- Direct marketing of educational programs
- Advertising and Promotion of Academic Programs and Institutions
- Marketing Theories within Education
- Academic Administration
- Faculty Administration and Management

IGI Global is currently accepting manuscripts for publication within this series. To submit a proposal for a volume in this series, please contact our Acquisition Editors at Acquisitions@igi-global.com or visit: http://www.igi-global.com/publish/.

The Advances in Educational Marketing, Administration, and Leadership (AEMAL) Book Series (ISSN 2326-9022) is published by IGI Global, 701 E. Chocolate Avenue, Hershey, PA 17033-1240, USA, www.igi-global.com. This series is composed of titles available for purchase individually; each title is edited to be contextually exclusive from any other title within the series. For pricing and ordering information please visit http://www.igi-global.com/book-series/advances-educational-marketing-administration-leadership/73677. Postmaster: Send all address changes to above address.

Titles in this Series

For a list of additional titles in this series, please visit:
https://www.igi-global.com/book-series/advances-educational-marketing-administration-leadership/73677

Funding Challenges and Successes in Arts Education
Siu Challons-Lipton (Queens University of Charlotte, USA) and Richard Emanuel (Alabama State University, USA)
Information Science Reference • ©2018 • 211pp • H/C (ISBN: 9781522525813) • US $170.00

Handbook of Research on Technology-Centric Strategies for Higher Education...
Purnendu Tripathi (Indira Gandhi National Open University (IGNOU), India) and Siran Mukerji (Indira Gandhi National Open University (IGNOU), India)
Information Science Reference • ©2017 • 501pp • H/C (ISBN: 9781522525486) • US $260.00

The Future of Accessibility in International Higher Education
Henry C. Alphin Jr. (Drexel University, USA) Roy Y. Chan (Indiana University, USA) and Jennie Lavine (University of Hull, UK)
Information Science Reference • ©2017 • 321pp • H/C (ISBN: 9781522525608) • US $195.00

Disability and Equity in Higher Education Accessibility
Henry C. Alphin, Jr. (Drexel University, USA) Jennie Lavine (University of Hull, UK) and Roy Y. Chan (Indiana University, USA)
Information Science Reference • ©2017 • 349pp • H/C (ISBN: 9781522526650) • US $190.00

Handbook of Research on Science Education and University Outreach as a Tool...
B. Pandu Ranga Narasimharao (Indira Gandhi National Open University IGNOU, India) Elizabeth Wright (Keck Graduate Institute (KGI), USA) Shashidhara Prasad (University of Mysore, India) and Meghana Joshi (Keck Graduate Institute (KGI), USA)
Information Science Reference • ©2017 • 370pp • H/C (ISBN: 9781522518808) • US $260.00

Deconstructing the Education-Industrial Complex in the Digital Age
Douglas Loveless (University of Auckland, New Zealand) Pamela Sullivan (James Madison University, USA) Katie Dredger (James Madison University, USA) and Jim Burns (Florida International University, USA)
Information Science Reference • ©2017 • 354pp • H/C (ISBN: 9781522521013) • US $195.00

For an enitre list of titles in this series, please visit:
https://www.igi-global.com/book-series/advances-educational-marketing-administration-leadership/73677

IGI Global
DISSEMINATOR OF KNOWLEDGE

701 East Chocolate Avenue, Hershey, PA 17033, USA
Tel: 717-533-8845 x100 • Fax: 717-533-8661
E-Mail: cust@igi-global.com • www.igi-global.com

Table of Contents

Preface

The development of an effective local workforce is imperative for the economic prosperity of a community. It focuses on the skills local businesses and industries require to yield successful outcomes in the community, and essentially can develop competitiveness in the global market (Haralson, 2010). Economic development that will affect the community, the state, or even the global market, drives business and industry, and requires a well-trained workforce to achieve goals for economic prosperity. Achieving a sustainable workforce calls for worker skills that match the demands of the local environment. Thus, workforce development matches the skills of workers with the demands of the workplace (Haralson, 2010). Workforce-education programs are well suited to students, because such programs partner with business and industry, and simultaneously offer specific training opportunities to guide students toward their career path. Workforce and technical programs provide easy access, quick payouts, and the ability to meet a variety of interests (Holzer, 2008). Enlisting the assistance of higher education to gain or retrain in a new skill will put the student on his/her way to achieving full potential as an active contributor to the economic growth of the society. A comprehensive approach to developing a local workforce means utilizing community connections, invested employers, industry-driven support, skilled training, and networking. Integrating a workforce development strategy builds on past efforts, using job strategies that include local training, support of employers, long-term and short-term specific skill-set training, and job-placement considerations (Haralson, 2010). Higher education prepares students to succeed in their chosen fields, and when it contributes to the development of a community workforce, it streamlines and organizes the multiple paths to workforce development, and provides workforce support effectively and efficiently.

This book focuses on the contention that advisory committees are essential for all workforce programs, and instrumental in providing funding, job placement, training, management, equipment, and support. It defines an advisory committee as a select group of leaders who provide knowledge and guidance to the development and continuity of a community's workforce program. The Texas Higher Education Coordinating Board mandates an advisory committee for community colleges; however, there are many advisory committees besides those in the field of education, created of their own accord. Across the nation, advisory committees in the areas of education and medicine are used to create better programs and proactively address issues. Advisory committees provide an educated and well-trained workforce with up-to-date practitioners, access to specialists, and input and advice from professionals in the field. Even though the medical field does not mandate the use of advisory committees in all areas, biomedical research and education use them to explore the best practices and guiding principles for successfully advancing a project. The exact roles they play in biomedical research differ between and within institutions. At institutions with biomedical research and education programs, an advisory committee provides counsel, advice, collaboration, and assessment of research projects. Their very existence helps to drive scientific endeavours toward positive outcomes. Biomedical research and education must establish relevant, diverse, collaborative, and engaging advisory committees that will advocate for the goals of these fields, such as advancing the objectives of furthering understanding, knowledge, associations, and technologies fundamental to improving health outcomes. Additionally, advisory committees play an important role in collaboration, and impact the development and management of research projects. The advisory committee has a variety of functions, including promoting programs to the community, offering suggestions for improving specific areas of the program, and assessment (Schaeffer & Rouse, 2014). Since each committee member has experience and expertise in the program area, the committee can offer the most current skills available (Schaeffer & Rouse, 2014). Whether at the level of colleges and universities or within employment, advisory committees assist with decision-making and recommendations. Even though they may operate at diverse levels and exist for various reasons, advisory committees are paramount to program success. The purpose of this discussion of advisory committees will narrow the conversation and focus mainly on community colleges that have mandated advisory committees and are increasingly beneficial to implement in biomedical education/research.

Advisory committees are crucial in collaborating and navigating successful outcomes in the fields of research and education. Biomedical research can generalize to a broader context the wide-ranging decision-making process that advisory committees in education use. Community-college regulations state that workforce-education programs make decisions through their advisory committees. To offset expenses, community colleges partner with local businesses in their community. Advisory committees serve as the heart of these partnerships, helping to combine resources, equipment, and knowledge in skilled areas. This book discusses the following issues related to advisory committees in biomedical research and education:

- Effective practices and strategies used by advisory committees related to biomedical research and education
- Equal representation and balance within advisory committees
- Addressing challenges to working collaboratively
- Lack of knowledge regarding advisory committees
- Participant perceptions about collaborative decision-making
- Networking opportunities
- Transparency

This discussion will explore best practices in the development of advisory committees in biomedical education and workforce development, and the guiding principles that result in successful research and opportunities.

This book will explore how the curriculum and concepts at the community college level and in higher education focus on improving necessary training in the medical community. The community college complements local workforce needs, and those of the country. Not only the students and the community utilize the strategic commitment to workforce needs; the United States utilizes its best practices to train and begin the process of developing future nurses and doctors. The medical community also makes strategic use of the advisory committee in workforce departments at the community college. To keep abreast of continual changes in the workforce, the advisory committee is the optimal way to utilize innovation and strategic practices at the community college and in the medical arena.

The discussion here will highlight how community colleges rely on their advisory committees to provide funding, equipment, and personal support. The decision-making process that community-college practitioners and workforce advisory-committee members use to make informed decisions is vital to the success of workforce-education programs. The need for collaborations between community-college workforce programs and business/industry is essential to offsetting the expense of operations. Continued budget cuts in higher education burden faculty, students, and programs; and a program's initial start-up is costly, absent partnering with business/industry. The advisory committee is central to successfully keeping workforce programs funded, equipment and internships available, and a healthy supply of community support intact.

Lack of effective decision-making in higher education will directly affect the success of workforce-education programs. Decision-making with business/industry is fundamentally sound, based on skill sets needed now and for years to come (Kilcrease, 2011), and characterized by perseverance, tenacity, consistency, and evaluation of the overall product. The key to making good decisions depends on knowing what to ask, how to ask it, and how to assess actual needs in a community (J. Cornett, personal communication, July 7, 2015). It comes down to confidence and belief in the ability to make decisions as a committee.

This discussion includes exploring how a strong, involved leader working cohesively with the advisory committee will affect the outcomes of a workforce-education program. Key individuals are important to a group trying to achieve a common goal, because they have the ability to influence others to follow directives. Leadership style can transform the advisory committee into a powerful asset, led by consultants and executives sharing their workforce-program experiences. Having enthusiastic and committed members on the advisory committee, along with experienced, articulate, and confident leadership, results in the overall success of workforce-education programs (Johnson, 2013; Meeder & Pawlowski, 2012). To create unity among the members, a strong leader will help them to see the benefits associated with making concessions and negotiating what best serves the workforce-education program (Burke & Miller, 1999; Johnson, 2013; Northouse, 2013). Including individuals with the ability to commit to a decision and a course of action creates stability on the committee (Mintzberg, 1979). Influential members in the community must serve on the committee and take an active role in leadership, including meeting with other business/industry members, to encourage donations of equipment and supplies to the programs. The reader of this book will benefit from the recommendations for seeking partnerships with business/industry, and taking advantage of how advisory committees can assist, as higher education continues to experience budget cuts.

Finally, the book will include a discussion of how higher education must collaborate with workforce advisory committees in decision-making. The collaborations established with workforce programs through their advisory committee provide direct access to current business/industry information, including skills needed in the changing workforce. The decision-making processes used in business and industry are based on years of experience, and shared among the advisory committee to support the workforce programs, through networking during advisory committee meetings and sharing information. Advisory committees should include networking as part of the decision-making process to help create progress, obtain resources, and develop public awareness of the training programs (Guidelines for Instructional Programs in Workforce Education [GIPWE], 2015; Texas Higher Education Coordinating Board [THECB], 2013).

AUDIENCE

This book will benefit various individuals and organizations, including not only community colleges, but also programs leading to higher education and the workforce. Community colleges, workforce programs, and medical areas utilize advisory committees. Whether they meet in a formal or an informal setting, the benefit of their input is critical to program success. The workforce is strategic and innovative when it uses collaborative partnerships to provide individuals in communities with training and retraining to compete in a changing workforce. This book will help institutions use advisory committees to the fullest, to bring about negotiations and partnerships to advance skills for workers.

This book focuses on the role of advisory committees in workforce education. Those who can benefit from the information presented include committee development officers, business/industry professionals, administrators, and workforce-education specialists. The collaborative nature of the partnerships within workforce-education programs creates opportunities to benefit for professionals in a variety of specializations.

The findings in this book can also benefit higher-education practitioners using decision-making skills. The decision-making process used in workforce-education programs requires collaborating with key individuals in local business/industry. Making accurate decisions by combining the expertise of key individuals with that of business/industry leaders leads to producing a quality workforce-education program.

ORGANIZATION OF THE BOOK

This book is comprised of six chapters that discuss the role of advisory committees in biomedical education and workforce development. Following is a brief overview of the chapters.

Chapter 1: Overview of Workforce Development in Education

This chapter highlights the history of workforce and technical programs in education, focusing on the multiple legislative acts that have played an integral part in training workers. The chapter also focuses on the alignment of workforce training to develop specific skill sets, joining workers with community needs through workforce training. Paying particular attention to advisory committees in community colleges and higher education, and the challenges facing today's workforce, this chapter focuses on the challenges that growing and evolving workforce faces, and how to train and retrain to keep pace with those changes.

Chapter 2: The Roles and Characteristics of Advisory Committees

This chapter explores the governance and roles of advisory committees, general advisory-committee characteristics, committee membership, what makes an effective committee, and how the committees function. The discussion includes the complex nature of the development and operation of workforce programs, and how workforce-education programs implement an industry-based advisory committee for guidance and support. This chapter also concentrates on the role of advisory committees and their characteristics, including who should be on the committee, and why they are important to the group dynamics and success of the committee.

Chapter 3: Decision-Making

This chapter focuses on the decision-making process and the dynamics of making successful decisions. Of particular interest are goals, equal representation, balance, consequences, leadership, harmony, and medical decision-making. This chapter explores the perceptions of and experiences with the decision-making process that community-college practitioners and workforce-education programs utilize—specifically, decision-making processes and the strategies used to enhance collaboration among stakeholders, especially those perceived to be best practices. This chapter discusses the practice of higher education and the body of knowledge used by community-college workforce advisory-committee members to make informed decisions for workforce-education programs.

Chapter 4: Advisory Committees in Biomedical Research and Training

Central to the development of biomedical research and training, is the formation and implementation of advisory committees that will assess the scientific training, education, project selection, and sponsorship that an institution provides. Advisory committees in biomedical research and training extend their assessments to a variety of areas in the training and research experience. They range from determination of institutional needs for maintaining competitive recruiting of quality trainees, curriculum development, and drafting of proposals to acquire federal grants for research training. Advisory committees are ubiquitous and necessary in biomedical research education and they are the basis for successful programs. In this chapter, the organization of advisory committees at different levels of biomedical research education and training is explored. Ranging from thesis advisory committees to institutional graduate education advisory committees.

Chapter 5: Development of a Biomedical Research Workforce

Various organizations are key stakeholders in biomedical research education and training, and their involvement and support are crucial at the training and education level, to enhance and produce an effective, competent, and engaging workforce. On many accounts, government, industry, and the general public hold critical opinions on project development and advancement, financial investment, and moral support. The participation of key stakeholders in advisory committees can positively drive the development of a biomedical research workforce. This chapter identifies and discusses the involvement of key stakeholders in biomedical research education and training, and alludes to the expectations that these entities can and should derive from their active engagement, in support of biomedical research education and training.

Chapter 6: Challenges to Working Collaboratively

This chapter recounts actual accounts of individuals currently working with advisory committees, their experiences and the lessons learned from those practices. The chapter includes discussions from practitioners regarding decision-making process, lack of knowledge, effects of business/industry on workforce programs, and advisory committees and best practices, offered by practitioners with years of experience, all of whom serve on advisory committees. It is important to gain perspective directly from business/industry and service providers through their own words and experiences, to create a complete outlook regarding the project and program under consideration.

Conclusion

This chapter serves as an overall conclusion to the book on advisory committees. Advisory committees are growing in popularity and recognition, whether they are used in medical, business, industry, or education the role of the committee is vital. The selection of proven decision-makers placed on the committee is important to the success. It is more important than ever to form efficient and effective advisory committees for all stakeholders involved. This book is written to provide suggestions and insights for creating, implementing, and generating a successful advisory committee.

CONCLUSION

Keeping informed of the ever-changing skill requirements and training required for employees is an ongoing challenge for workforce development. The same is true in the field of biomedical research and education. The information in this book will help higher-education administrators, deans, department chairs, faculty, and business/industry to understand the workings of advisory committees, and the potential benefits for the institution of implementing the committee. The collaborative practice described in *The Role of Advisory Committees in Biomedical Education and Workforce Development* encourages practitioners to use advisory committees for guidance, support, supplies, networking, internships, knowledge, donations, and to work together, sharing knowledge and ideas to strengthen their programs. Biomedical research education and workforce is, on many accounts, a powerful enterprise that drives the health, welfare, economy, technology, and social outcomes in local and global communities. The research and educational practices at these institutions have the potential to improve health outcomes, diversify opportunities, decrease knowledge gaps, increment technology, and improve workforce preparation and transition.

A novel area for further research and analysis, which is well beyond the preparation of this publication, is the impact in the development of commercialization opportunities within institutions providing biomedical research education. Many biomedical research institutions seek to develop technologies that can be commercialized to the industrial sector, and thus can contribute to the development of entrepreneurship and workforce enhancement and expansion. Advisory committees that are able to aptly represent different participating entities: such as trainees, principal investigators, institutional administrators, industrial representatives, and outside investors, will benefit in obtaining funding venues, targeting opportunities for collaboration, and delivering expedient outcomes to assess the development of new technologies.

Advisory committees are well utilized in biomedical research education and training, but there is an under value and underutilization in assisting and providing workforce development. Considering the investment in the training and preparation of biomedical research trainees, it would be wise to facilitate opportunities and develop committees, groups, facilities that collaborate with additional stakeholders to improve transitional outcomes from education to the workforce.

REFERENCES

Burke, L., & Miller, M. (1999). Taking the mystery out of intuitive decision-making. Retrieved from http://aspnet.cob.ohio.edu/mc/pmba_co_3/Class/ CMBA602Strategic/ TheMaterialReadings/ Module%202%20 Readings/R%234%20Taking% 20the%20Mystery% 20out%20of% 20Intuitive %20Decision%20Making.pdf.

GIPWE. (2010, 2015). Guidelines for instructional workforce education. Texas Higher Education Coordinating Board.

Haralson, L. (2010). What is workforce development? *Federal Reserve Bank of St. Lewis*. Retrieved from https://www.stlouisfed.org/Publications/Bridges/Spring-2010/What-is-Workforce-Development#fn1

Holzer, H. J. (2008). Workforce training: What works? Who benefits? Retrieved from http://www.familyimpactseminars.org/s_wifis28c02.pdf

Holzer, H. J. (2010). Connecting people to work. Retrieved from https://www.brookings.edu/wp-content/uploads/2016/06/polarization_jobs_policy_holzer.pdf

Johnson, L. (2013). Bridging the gap between education and workforce. Retrieved from http://www.ascd.org/publications/newsletters/policy-priorities/vol20/num03/Career-Readines

Kilcrease, K. M. (2011). Faculty perceptions of business advisory boards: The challenge for effective communication. *Journal of Education for Business*, *86*(2), 78–83. doi:10.1080/08832323.2010.480989

Meeder, H. & Pawlowski, B. (2012). Building advisory boards that matter. Techniques, 2(28).

Mintzberg, H. (1979). *The structuring of organizations*. Upper Saddle River, NJ: Prentice Hall.

Northouse, P. G. (2013). *Leadership: Theory and practice*. Los Angeles, CA: Sage Publishing.

Schaeffer, D., & Rouse, D. (2014). Effective academic advisory committee relationships. *Contemporary issues in education research*. Retrieved from http://files.eric.ed.gov/fulltext/EJ1073283.pdf

Texas Higher Education Coordinating Board. (2013). *Advisory Boards*. Retrieved from http://www.thecb.state.tx.us/index.cfm?objectid=8C1EF7E7-A71E-47E6-53FE5EFA82F38

Chapter 1
Overview of Workforce Development in Education

Julie Neal
Independent Researcher, USA

ABSTRACT

Workforce development focuses on economic development to boost a region's economic stability and prosperity, focusing on individuals. It is also described as the ability to sustain a workforce that can support current and future business/industry. Workforce and technical programs provide training in specialized fields to educate and prepare students to enter the workforce. Keeping in mind that business/industry requires trained employees, and employees need business/industry to create a sustainable lifestyle, decision-makers with knowledge and skills to lead their company and employees in a sustainable, prosperous direction are also required. This chapter explores workforce-development advisory committees, focusing on their relationship with community colleges and higher education. A particular focus is on the challenges growing and evolving workforce faces, and how to train and retrain to keep up with a changing and emerging workforce.

BACKGROUND

Higher education utilizes several terms to denote vocational education. These include terminal, vocational, occupational, career, technical, and workforce education (Cohen & Kisker, 2010; Cohen, Brawer, Kisker, 2013). Prior to the 1940s, the term vocational denoted programs in agriculture, trades, and

DOI: 10.4018/978-1-5225-4083-0.ch001

sales (Cohen & Kisker, 2010; Cohen et al., 2014). In the 1940s, the term terminal included all studies, other than baccalaureate, leading to employment (Cohen & Kisker, 2010; Cohen et al., 2014). The vocational programs were known as career education in the 1950s, geared toward younger students to acclimate them to future work, encompassing occupational and career studies (Cohen & Kisker, 2010; Cohen et al., 2013). Vocational education was initially considered a necessary part of a student's education, and for those students not seeking a terminal degree, the two-year college offered skills training that was more advanced than skills they had learned in high school (American Association of Community Colleges [AACC], 2013; Cohen et al., 2013; Cohen & Kisker, 2010).

Workforce and technical programs provide training in specialized fields to educate and prepare students to enter the workforce (Hodges, 2012). For purposes of this discussion, workforce education is the term used to identify these programs at two-year institutions. Workforce education has been an integral part of the community-college curriculum since 1862 (Cohen et al., 2013; Library of Congress, 2010). In the 20th century, the expectation of community colleges was to train workers so that the U.S. would have a supply of skilled employees for industry (Cohen et al., 2013). Workforce education in the U.S. evolved through the Morrill Act of 1862, which allowed colleges to use the proceeds from federal land sales to establish institutions (AACC, 2014; Cohen & Kisker, 2010; Library of Congress, 2010). Colleges focused on agriculture and mechanical arts, and the act created the first workforce-education initiative (Cohen & Kisker, 2010; Library of Congress, 2010).

In the 1950s and 1960s, workforce education was considered only for those students who needed or wanted to complete formal trade schooling in order to be eligible to join the workforce (Cohen et al., 2014; Cohen & Kisker, 2010). Since the 1970s, it has become common practice for students who complete their workforce programs to transfer to baccalaureate studies. This is due in part to the development of articulation agreements (Beach, 2011; Cohen et al., 2014; Cohen & Kisker, 2010). Articulation agreements are partnerships between community colleges and four-year colleges or universities whereby certain courses taken at a community college are transferable to the four-year institution (Cohen et al., 2014; Cohen & Kisker, 2010).

From the 1960s through the 1980s, workforce education programs grew faster in community colleges than liberal-arts programs did, due to many factors (Cohen et al., 2014). These factors included the early leadership of the community-college movement in developing a focus on training students for the workplace. Other contributions to this growth included the Vocational

Education Act of 1963 and its amendments; changing labor markets; increased enrollments of part-time students other than white, elite males; and absorption of adult education and occupational programs from secondary schools (Cohen et al., 2013). Cohen et al. (2013) also identify multiple legislative acts that affected the growth of workforce education in the U.S.:

- The Vocational Education Act in 1963
- The Vocational Education Act Amendments in 1968 and 1972
- The creation of the Comprehensive Employment & Training Act in 1973
- The Job Training Act in 1982
- The Carl D. Perkins Vocational Education Act in 1984

The federal Vocational Education Act of 1963 and its subsequent amendments have had significant impact on workforce-education programs in community colleges. The act provided additional federal funds to community colleges to aid workforce programs, work-study programs, business education, educational classes, and research (Cohen et al., 2013). Congress approved the Vocational Education Act in order to align training with the needs of industry and business (Cohen et al., 2013). In 1968 and 1972, Congress approved additional funds through amendments to this act, which provided additional support for workforce-education programs, including training for students with disabilities (Cohen et al., 2013). The act redirected a major portion of funding to workforce-education programs in order to train and, in some cases, retrain students in skilled areas, especially in areas of technology (Vocational Education Act, 1963). In addition, the act also requires states to change and upgrade workforce training to coincide with economic demands and to compete globally (Cohen et al., 2013).

The history of workforce development has included much significant legislation, including the Workforce Investment Act (WIA) of 1998, providing job-training, education, and employment services to local communities, and giving authority to state and local governments to tailor their own job-training programs (Workforce Development Overview, [WDO], 2012). The WIA utilized seven key principles for structuring workforce development: streamlining and integration, empowering individuals, universal access, increased accountability, strategic planning and oversight, flexibility, and youth activities (WDO, 2012). The WIA of 1998 was legislation introduced under President Clinton for "one-stop" delivery of workforce services (LaRose, 2014).

According to the Texas Higher Education Coordinating Board (2013), when referring to educational programs, the terms technical and workforce are interchangeable and will be used in that accord. Each community college district uses its own terminology to refer to particular programmatic offerings. Typically, workforce courses are considered continuing education, while technical courses are considered credit hours, require strict compliance as set out in the GIPWE manual, and are possibly transferrable to four-year institutions under articulation agreements (wherein students move seamlessly from one institution to another, with university partnerships).

WORKFORCE DEVELOPMENT

A particular characteristic of community colleges is that they offer a diverse range of workforce-education programs that impact the economy. These programs are designed to train students and individuals with specific hands-on skills that enable them to enter directly into the workforce (Hamilton, 2004; Kress, 2012). A study conducted by Kazis (2011), as part of the Brookings-Rockefeller Project, suggests that community college and workforce collaborations are crucial to sustainable economic development. Aligning job training with current economic workforce needs will generate significant numbers of employed workers, specifically in middle-skill jobs; develop a highly-qualified labor supply; and help contribute to a long-term supply of workers and a strong, sustainable economy (Baber, 2011; Hodges, 2012; Kazis, 2011). Accomplishing this goal requires alignment of regional needs with workforce needs, and a workforce-education program designed to provide this needed training (Hodges, 2012). The findings of the Brookings-Rockefeller Project indicate a need to streamline current certificate programs at community colleges, to achieve stronger economic payoffs (Kazis, 2011) by more quickly producing graduates, through the restructuring of programs into more flexible modes of delivery, such as weekend courses, block courses, and courses delivered online.

Through their workforce-education programs, community colleges work closely with business and industry employers to identify needed workforce skills, and design a training program led by the college that will create a feasible solution to providing trained workers (American Association of Community Colleges [AACC] and National Center on Education and the Economy [NCEE], 2009). Workforce-education programs create coursework matching the needs of business and industry, leading to certificates, permits, degrees, and ultimately employment for the student (AACC & NCEE, 2009). Businesses and industry working with community colleges is part of an effort to put Americans back to work in needed skilled areas, to help the economy (Carlson, Holm & Uvalde, 2011). Individual businesses do not have the funds or skills necessary to train, conduct research, and market all their needs, especially when competing globally (American College Testing [ACT], 2012); Carlson et al., 2011; Soares, 2010). According to Carlson et al. (2011), business and industry leaders have realized that combining efforts to train workers results in an effective economic gain from sharing materials, supplies, equipment, and services. These scholars have found that economic-development organizations, working with education, government agencies, and training providers, collaborate effectively to develop and identify new market areas, and train the needed workers with access to specialized technology and information (e.g., Carlson et al., 2011). In addition, they suggest allowing the invested stakeholders in the area to be instrumental in the decision-making process, in order to ward off too much control by any one entity, which could impede progress.

Workforce programs increase and deepen the relationships between business/industry and the community, while also creating a vested interest among the local citizenry (Carlson, 2011). This creates a rapport with employers and prospective employees and requires a commitment with business/industry in the area (Carlson, 2011). Increasingly, business/industry are collaborating with local community members to develop curriculum and training programs that lead to potential student internships in their business, and future employment (Carlson, 2011). When developing workforce programs, including local business owners, administrators, and managers on advisory committees helps ensure potential employment for the students; resources to help run an efficient program; and guidance for the overall benefit of the program. The advisory committee is the vital component serving as the key to negotiations in developing and implementing programs, training, and curriculum in workforce and technical areas of instruction (Hodges, 2012).

In order to provide the country with a continual supply of skilled workers, community colleges, in collaboration with businesses and industries, lead to improved student success and economic progress (Kazis, 2011). Workforce programs at the community college are an approach to enhancing economic stability and creating prosperity for citizens, as well as businesses. The programs are problem-centered approaches to addressing shortages in skilled labor, and generate a trained supply of skilled workers in particular areas of need in a region. The workforce programs are designed to link employee training and specific techniques, to match the needs of business/industry already established in an area or wanting to expand into the region. Workforce programs link employee training with community resources, through partnerships to provide a constant supply of trained workers.

Workforce and technical programs are gaining popularity, because they offer students specialized training and critical skills needed for employment (Hamilton, 2004). The goal of workforce development is to provide citizens with relevant training and skills to make them employable immediately upon completion of the program (Carlson et al., 2011). To offset the expense associated with workforce programs, advisory committees serve as the heart of business and industry partnerships, helping to combine resources, equipment, and knowledge in skilled areas (Greenstone & Looney, 2011; Holzer, 2008). For example, New York City has developed a new career pathway framework to align career paths with competitive markets, instead of the prior rationale of training workers as quickly as possible and just placing them with employers (González-Rivera, 2016). The new design takes recommendations from stakeholders—employers, businesses, labor unions, educational institutions, and local government officials. New York City has refocused the workforce development system to create a deeper connection with the stakeholders sharing ideas and resources. New York City is committed to helping individuals to acquire middle-income jobs by helping them develop the specific skills needed to move into these positions (González-Rivera, 2016). The city is also committed to overhauling its workforce development in order to meet the labor demands of the 21st century. A modern workforce market constantly requires workers to retrain and upgrade their training, to stay relevant in a demanding job market. New York City realizes a relevant workforce development system is a necessary strategy to ensure workers' skills are kept current, necessary to earn a good living (Gonzalez-Rivera, 2016). Workers who do not receive upgrades in training will be hard pressed to find employment that allows them to enjoy a decent living, especially in a large area like New York City. Unfortunately, training and upgrading skills can be expensive and time consuming, a major hindrance to those workers categorized as middle income or lower. Therefore, New York City workforce development is partnering with business and industry, as well as other city agencies, pooling their funds to ultimately provide training to workers in areas of demand (González-Rivera, 2016). The city is also upgrading technology and communication with other departments, to accommodate and match individuals with training and skills across the city. The city realizes workers must be placed in employment as quickly as possible, with little down time. The workforce development program gives credit for alternative learning, so that students and workers receive credit toward their degree, and credentials for hours spent through partnerships, summer work, high-school classes, internships, workshops, and advanced learning. The City of New York is going through the process of upgrading and making necessary changes to its workforce-development programs. Yet, stakeholders understand that change is difficult and requires an obligation from all involved to commit for the long haul. Therefore, New York City workforce development is partnering with business and industry, as well as other city agencies, pooling their funds to ultimately provide training to workers in areas of demand (González-Rivera, 2016). The city is also upgrading technology and communication with other departments, to accommodate and match individuals with training and skills across the city. The city realizes workers must be placed in employment as quickly as possible, with little down time. The workforce development program gives credit for alternative learning, so that students and workers receive credit toward their degree, and credentials for hours spent through partnerships, summer work, high-school classes, internships, workshops, and advanced learning. The City of New York is going through the process of upgrading and making necessary changes to its workforce-development programs. Yet, stakeholders understand that change is difficult and requires an obligation from all involved to commit for the long haul.

As in New York City, workforce on-the-job training or work-related training – depending on how it is defined—can be delivered through diverse formats, such as workshops, seminars, lectures, distance education, internships, and on-the-job training provided by business and industry (Cronen & Murphy, 2013). Educators working closely with business and industry will be able to obtain a measurement of the accurate enrollment in training, and an accurate description of work-related continuing job training and workforce needs, to enable educators to provide advanced training in these areas of need. The American Institute for Research (2013) reports the most widespread advanced training in the areas of business (35%), health (32%), and technical computer skills (15%), regardless of the provider, are currently areas with employee shortages (Cronen & Murphy, 2013). To bring partnerships to fruition and make the necessary and correct adjustments, an advisory committee is paramount to success. Advisory committees can share the latest initiatives, trends, and resources in the way of funds, equipment, job placement, training, knowledge, and experts in the field.

ADVISORY COMMITTEE AND THE COMMUNITY COLLEGE

Students are enrolling at community colleges and seeking specific training in the area of workforce and technical programs, realizing that the overall training for each program is relatively short, ranging from weeks to months, and well-paying jobs are available upon program completion (Carlson et al., 2011). The popularity of the workforce and technical programs for students is leading to more money over a lifetime for the students, as a result of the training they are receiving. In the long run, the student is less likely to experience unemployment, which benefits both students and employers (Carlson et al., 2011). This trend is expected to continue to grow for the next decade (Carlson et al., 2011).

The community college provides training for students in specialized areas of the workforce to support business and industry demands. This practice dates back to 1957, when junior colleges identified the vocational-technical needs they could satisfy to fulfill society's workforce shortages (Cohen et al., 2013). As society demands specialized skills and knowledge for employees seeking jobs, community colleges are adapting to changing demands of the workforce and providing a range of diverse programs (Cohen et al., 2013). Many of these positions are high paying, resulting in higher personal income for the country's citizens, contributing to the overall good of the economy (Cohen et al., 2013).

Training students with particular skills is expensive, and the community college carries most of the cost. Industry leaders must be willing to partner with community colleges, and acknowledge their share of training expenses, as colleges are growing rapidly and budgets are stretched to cover expansion throughout the organization (National Center for Education Statistics) [NCES], 2010). Cohen et al. (2013) suggest opening channels to merge public and private funds, so that an equitable share is borne by each. An advisory committee (in some instances known as an advisory board) utilizes a best-practices approach, including research, technology, experiences, and consulting, to improve and develop healthcare and educational programs (Texas State Library [TSL], 2016). Workforce leadership has evolved from one owner making all the decisions, to the complex system now in place, known as the advisory committee, which enlists experts and local citizenry in sharing ideas to benefit the student, the program, the community, and the economy.

The community college has become a bonding agent for the workforce, economic development, business and industry, and collaborative partnerships. The college is providing key services in the areas of agriculture, automotive advancement, building trades, carpentry, certified nurse's aides (CNAs), computer skills, electrical, farm and ranch management, flight training, oilfield chemicals, oilfield safety, restaurant management, transportation, trucking, welding, and wind energy. Business and industry are partnering with community colleges in a proactive effort to fund and provide trainers to upgrade worker skills, improve services by being more efficient, increase employment opportunities in the area, reduce cost of outcomes, and become self-sufficient as a community. These targeted careers account for 23% of all projected job openings between 2008 and 2018 (ACT, 2012).

Workforce programs have been known to increase the relationships between the college and the community, as well as to create an increase in equity of the citizens in a community (Carlson, 2011). Workers are able to increase their skills and compete for high-paying jobs in a specific region. The community college has the ability to change rapidly to respond to upcoming trends, and remove programs that become obsolete in an area. All in all, this requires a substantiated rapport with business and industry in the area where the college is located. The college networks and partners with local businesses to develop curriculums and allow potential workers to intern within the business. This creates a link between employers and potential employees. Including local business owners, chief executive officers (CEOs), and managers on advisory committees will help to ensure potential employment for the students, resources to help run an efficient program, and guidance for the overall benefit of the program.

Businesses competing globally require more specialized training to meet the rising standards in technical industries. Greater knowledge and skills are being demanded of the labor market, and colleges, as well as business and industry, are being asked to do more to prepare individuals for this changing workforce (Perna, 2012). The collaborative efforts of colleges with business and industry to develop funding, vision, corporate investment, goals, and shared resources nurture result-driven practices to improve workers' skills and build stronger communities (Baber, 2011; Heitman, 2005). Therefore, an even greater need has developed for informed and active advisory members within workforce programs. These members will be called upon to help identify specific skill traits. As the ACT (2016) reports, "job profiling" – matching skills to jobs—requires identifying what is needed in the workforce area, and then matching the student's skill sets to identify what further training is required. The first step is for the employers to identify what skills jobs require. Second, each individual will assess his or her skills and match them with the job specifications. Third, the educational institutions, working with the employers, assess the prospective employees' skill levels, and prescribe specific training to enhance their employability (ACT, 2016).

Due to the job-profiling report findings, a strong need has arisen for a specifically trained workforce. Currently, the areas of carpentry, plumbing, pharmacy, construction, certified nurse's aides, commercial truck driving, computer technology, and automotive are just a few of the growing skill sets needed across the country. These programs offer easy access to training, with quick return on educational investment, and meet emerging career demands (Carlson et al., 2011; Holzer, 2008; Kazis, 2011). The job profiling occurs at all job skill levels. Some programs require only a minimal amount of training or retraining through certification, weekend refresher courses, or a longer associates program. Additional training is available in the educational spectrum to continue to even greater skill levels, with a bachelor's degree, and even at the university research level. The educational workforce is designed to match each individual with the appropriate skill level and placement in employment, while at the same time offering even greater opportunities to train in areas requiring high-level skills.

The increasing demand for specially trained workers within businesses and industries has resulted in an increasing need for a skilled workforce. The U.S. Department of Labor (2016) estimates 7 million jobs will require skilled laborers by 2024. Historically, community colleges are the institutions on which business and industry rely to provide programs tailored to the industries' needs as they emerge. The community college can be the stepping-stone for students to further their education, and go on to more training in higher education at the university level. Many medical positions begin in the community college—Licensed Vocational Nursing (LVN), pharmacy tech, physician's assistant, dental assistant, and vet techs—and then continue on to specific areas as registered nurses, pharmacists, doctors, dentists, and veterinarians.

STATEMENT OF THE CHALLENGES

Workforce development focuses on putting individuals in society to work. Whether it is manual labor, management, or doctoral-level employment, there is a job for each individual. Training is available at all levels and for most, if not all, skill requirements. One interesting challenge for workforce development is keeping up with the ever-changing demands for specific skills. This includes retraining for current employees, to meet up-to-date requirements, or going back to school to enter a management or higher-level position. The education sector is trained and equipped to meet workforce-training needs, whether at certificate, associates, bachelor, or post-baccalaureate levels. Similarly, the oilfield industry, like medical fields, is known for creating jobs. Whenever the oil industry is expanding in an area, jobs become available in all areas of the workforce, houses and apartments are in demand, new restaurants and facilities are built, infrastructures require updating, and more emergency clinics open, with doctors, nurses, aides, and support personnel. Advancement in the industry is readily available and, importantly, the oilfield is generous with donations to education and retraining. For example, oilfield corporation Baker Hughes wants to make a positive community impact through contributions at the corporate, regional, and geomarket levels. In 2014, Baker Hughes contributed about $3 million for improvements in the areas of education, health, youth, and culture (Baker Hughes, 2016). Their goal is to build economic well-being in communities, and be responsive to their social needs (Baker Hughes, 2016). Chesapeake Energy, Halliburton, and Chevron, just to name a few, have histories of donating to education and communities also. A comparable situation exists in the medical field. With a medical facility in an area, more jobs are available at all levels of employment; retraining and advancement within the industry is common; opportunity exist for LVNs to continue training to become RNs; and the aforementioned economic advances resemble those seen with the oil industry. Substantial growth within the medical field sustains and accommodates workers, resulting in economic growth. Just as in the oil industry, generous donations are prevalent in the medical field. In 2011, MD Anderson received a donation of $150 million, the largest monetary gift to the institution (Destefano, 2011). Donations to both the medical field and business/industry are a major part of what helps these institutions to stay afloat, and to change and grow as their particular business keeps up with an ever-progressing society.

In the state of Texas, several metropolitan areas, such as Houston, San Antonio, Dallas, and Fort Worth, are home to expansive medical centers, and oil and gas headquarters. As mentioned above, these industries bring in jobs from across the country, as well as advancements in technology and economic development. Looking at these areas to set the standard for workforce direction should be advantageous. For example, in Texas, even though unemployment is decreasing, newly emerging training is needed.

The Texas Workforce Commission has reported that unemployment rates decreased for the second consecutive month in 2016, to 3.6% (McEwen, 2016). Specifically, Workforce Solutions of the Permian Basin area saw a 1,000-job increase for October and November of 2016, in the areas of trade, transportation, and utilities (McEwen, 2016). Workforce area training programs at the three local colleges (Midland, Howard, and Odessa) reported classes at full capacity. The demand for a skilled workforce is growing so rapidly that there is a concern that technological advances may begin to replace some of the workforce jobs. In the Permian Basin area, where oilfield technology leads the way in current trends for the oil and gas industry, some predict with concern that automation and technology will take the place of jobs (Blum, 2016). Emergent trends in the area of drilling will appear next year in the Permian Basin area, as drilling rigs become more and more advanced with the use of sophisticated software. Prospective employees are apprehensive that modern advances will replace their jobs. For instance, energy analyst Byron Pope, from Houston, projected that up to 40% fewer jobs will be needed in the oilfield, according to research from Tudor, Pickering, Holt & Co. (Blum, 2016). Blum (2016) reports that 215,000 jobs were lost within the last two years, with the downturn in the oil and gas industry; of these, many will not become available again as the industry gains strength. Jobs are being replaced with automation to eliminate human error and dangerous positions (Pope, 2016; Wethe, 2017). As drilling rigs become more efficient through automation, it is common to see rig hands replaced by laptops, not only in offices, but also in the fields (Wethe, 2017). Companies have tightened their spending and moved to greater effectiveness with a mix of labor and technology (Wethe, 2017). System engineers are designing automated systems that create efficiency in the oil and gas industry with the press of a button from office computers, equating to additional savings for business and industry (Wethe, 2017). The impact of technology on the oil and gas industry is just one example of how it is leading the way for new areas of training and retraining. Considering this information, it is more important than ever that business and industry utilize workforce training and retraining programs to focus on the skill demands required for up-and-coming advances, in technology and other emerging areas.

In answer to the possibility of job loss, Brandon Spencer, vice-president of ABB Technologies, explained that the heavy reliance on automation did not necessarily mean a reduction in the job force, and could mean an opportunity to retrain more highly skilled technical workers (Blum, 2016). Bear in mind that the term Spencer used— "highly skilled"—equates to "specifically trained" in today's workforce. Once again, community colleges will find themselves under more pressure (including more expense) to keep up with the demand for relevant training that shadows workforce demands. To navigate these advances, the advisory committees function as consultants to inform, direct, and advance business and industry, colleges, and communities. To help advise the community colleges, they will turn to utilizing the members of the advisory committees for their insight and real-world applicable knowledge, to inform institutions and program committees of the advancements and skills that will be needed. It is more important than ever to wisely consider who is on the committee, and utilize networking to include individuals with the greatest knowledge in particular skill areas.

Another emergent trend in technology arises in the form of increasing online purchasing. According to the Wall Street Journal, some traditional retailers, including Macy's and Sears, are closing stores that will be replaced by the tech industry (Stevens, 2016). Yet, on the other end of the spectrum, Amazon reported it would hire over 100,000 employees as the industry continues using innovation as its guiding principal (Stevens, 2016). Even though jobs were lost by the traditional brick and mortar stores as society's hurry-up, no-time lifestyle emerged, new possibilities and jobs in the areas of cloud technology, machine learning, and advanced logistics will soon be available, and will require training. Since Amazon's plans to open new facilities in Texas, California, Florida, and New Jersey will also mean economic growth in those areas, providing services for all the new employees will stimulate the economy in those areas of new business (Stevens, 2016). This appears to be the new standard in modern society—employees needing to retrain more rapidly for new positions, as new technology and advances in logistics replace antiquated systems.

A telephone interview was conducted on January 4, 2017, with an oilfield employee who manages a software program that controls wells remotely (personal communication, January 4, 2017). He discussed modernization and technology in the workforce. He has 41 years of experience in the Permian Basin area of Texas, and 18 years with his present company. At the outset, he explained that he had encountered resistance to modernization and technology, only to gain the trust and respect of members in the oil and gas industry, once he proved that his product saved costs, improved production, and provided safety to employees. He now monitors around 580 wells for five different companies daily, since the wells can be accurately monitored remotely. In contrast, a field pumper could only physically monitor a fraction of the total wells remotely monitored, approximately 100 wells in two days as opposed to the 580 remotely monitored wells. This particular program monitors wells globally wherever there is Internet access, including Canada. The technology and modernization did not take jobs away, but changed and added to employee job descriptions, in addition to opening up areas for retraining in technology workforce areas. Training in the oilfield area of technology and engineering is conducive to providing upper-levels training in the two-year colleges and four-year universities. The modernization will require a deeper knowledge through specific skill sets, especially in the area of analysts, monitors, data-measurement technicians, and computer analysts (M. Dearing, personal communication, January 2, 2017). Analysts are reading the data in real time using automated systems generated by the progress in technology, which need trained workers to analyze and understand the information (M. Dearing, personal communication, January 2, 2017). The automation is consistently found in complex drilling rigs and offshore drilling. Dearing explained that additional training is also required to comply with more sophisticated emission regulations. Even though modernization is expensive, the benefits of safety and efficiency far outweigh the costs (M. Dearing, personal commination, January 2, 2017). Looking to the oilfield industry as a gauge, because it consists of a wealth of trained individuals that feed other industries, the oil and gas industry provides job opportunities from manual worker all the way to chief executive officer. The oilfield is known for the latest technical advances, hiring, providing new job opportunities, and paying well.

Doug Shapiro, Executive Research Director of the National Student Clearinghouse Research Center, reports that this progressive change in the workforce will continue to challenge educational institutions throughout the planning process required to adjust to the new changes (Korn, 2016). Encouraging reports by Ahmed Hashmi, head of Global Technologies for British Petroleum, explain that by 2035, the world will require 35% more energy, with the majority coming from the oil and gas industry (Blum, 2016). New jobs will emerge, which will require retraining within the workforce pool. It will fall to the guidance of the workforce advisory committee to plan a curriculum; set up field training, internships, and access to new equipment; and identify trainers for these new advanced skills. This is good news for two-year, and especially four-year institutions, which have experienced declines in enrollment. However, even with the high cost of tuition, students who know there will be a return on their educational investment of future employment will find investing in their future worthwhile.

According to the report by the World Economic Forum (WEF), businesses will need to work closely with educational institutions and others to provide a skilled workforce to match 21st century employment needs (WEF, 2016). With advances in technology and workforce demands come opportunities for two-year and four-year educational institutions. For example, the aforementioned changes and new requirements in the oilfield will require engineers and technologists at varying levels of expertise. Not only does this apply to the oilfield; the same can be said of the medical field. The two workforce providers, medicine and oil/gas, are similar in their structure, as they hire many workers at all levels and from across the country. They also pride themselves on the latest advances and research in their respective fields, and provide economic advancement in areas where they locate.

ADVISORY COMMITTEE IN HIGHER EDUCATION

The four-year university operates under a complex system. While some advisory committees meet requirements set by accrediting agencies, others are voluntary (Rouse & Schaeffer, 2014). At the university level, a Board of Trustees, or Regents, has decision-making authority. Individual academic schools, departments, or programs may form an advisory committee (Rouse &Schaeffer, 2014). The committee may also be long-term or short-term need, depending on the problem or task. At the university level, if the program is budgeted above two million dollars, the institution must receive the Texas Higher Education Coordinating Board's approval; any amount under two million does not need approval from THECB, and the institution makes decisions (THECB, 2017). The Board of Regents makes decisions regarding educational programs, and functions under state mandates from the department of education and coordinating board. The system works from top-down regulation to bottom-up suggestions and recommendations, based on a formal hierarchy: State Department of Education or State Coordinating Board, Board of Regents, President or Chancellor, Department Deans, Department Heads, and then faculty. Each institution may establish an advisory committee or board as the need arises (THECB, 2017). The information is passed on to the faculty senate and moves up to the department dean, continuing up the chain as warranted. The advisory committees and boards are only created and exist when they are needed to help develop and make specific recommendations. Fundamentally, the Faculty Senate in higher education operates similarly to an advisory committee at the community-college level. However, the community-college advisory committees operate under a directive for all workforce programs to formally use advisory committees, as guided by the

GIPWE Manual. The Higher Education Faculty Senate consists of senior members of the institution's faculty, while advisory committees do not include full-time faculty, in order to make sure the committee's decisions are not biased.

In recent years, the general construct of educational boards has become more strategic, with greater comprehension of institutional operations (Pelletier, 2012). Members are recruited for their specific skill range in business and industry, especially for their particular expertise. At the university level, board members are not only experts in their field, but also aware of the institution's finances and commitments from stakeholders (Pelletier, 2012). The institution wants to align financial practices with best practices. Committee members must tailor their questions to their task, while keeping them consistent with the institution's mission (Pelletier, 2012). The higher-education committee members are often on other board committees, in order to fully understand the process and take ownership of their decisions. Most importantly, the higher-education committee should have a specific function and a set of responsibilities well thought out and understood by the members (Pelletier, 2012).

The Texas Higher Education Coordinating Board recognizes and utilizes advisory committees, referred to as advisory boards, at the four-year institution level; however, the member structure and purpose differs from those of the community-college workforce advisory committees. The higher-education advisory board includes members of the faculty, administrators from across the state's community- and technical-college programs, to identify and recommend to the Coordinating Board the courses that are acceptable for transfer to a general academic in height-level institution (THECB, 2016). Workforce education programs are typically short-term training, in the form of certificates or associate degrees, and the advisory committee consists of individuals within the workforce. In higher education, an advisory board (committee) is implemented upon need, and ceases to exist once its task is completed. It has no authority to act on its decisions, but does make recommendations. The advisory committee helps to make recommendations, to assist with community needs where seamless training does not exist. Even though there is no formal mandate to form committee or state rules, the advisory committee basically includes individuals within the community, with firsthand experience in the area of need. Like the community-college workforce programs, the state mandates advisory committees in the medical areas. For example, the American Journal of Preventive Medicine (2016) utilizes advisory committees for discussions and decision-making concerning immunization practices. Using evidence-based decision-making, the advisory committee sets the vaccination criteria and schedule (Lu, 2016). Likewise, a federal advisory committee provides external advice and guidance regarding preventable disease vaccines, using a well-rounded and representative committee consisting of doctors, disease-control organizations, and administrators, to make recommendations for disease control (Prevention and Control of Influenza with Vaccines [PCIV], 2016). Practitioners must be open to changes and compromise through the communication their advisory committees provide. Being open to change is not exclusive only to the medical field, but occurs in all areas of the workforce.

In an effort to create a competitive and talented workforce, the Business-Higher Education Forum (BHEF) is researching factors that contribute to higher-education partnerships and workforce programs (2013). The BHEF demonstrates how an advisory board (committee) is dedicated as an organization to addressing education and workforce challenges. BHEF is one of the oldest organizations represented by senior executives (composed of Fortune 500 CEOs, college and university presidents, and other knowledgeable regional leaders), which addresses global competitive issues. Its goal is to help align education and the workforce with innovation, so as to be economically competitive (BHEF, 2013). The BHEF studies groundbreaking communities that have advanced from business and education partnerships. A specific case study at the University of Houston's (UH) undergraduate program revealed that leaders in the energy industry, located in Houston, rapidly and successfully created an undergraduate program in petroleum engineering. Houston is considered to be the energy capital of the world, with approximately half of the economy connected to the energy industry (BHEF, 2013). Consequently, since Houston has around 40,000 jobs and 3,600 energy-driven companies based in Houston, the community believed a strong undergraduate petroleum-engineering program was needed (BHEF, 2013). The university realized the potential a partnership with business and industry would have for starting and sustaining a new petroleum-engineering degree. The partnership between higher education and the workforce demonstrated the combined effect in higher education and the community. BHEF attributes the success of the program to the advisory board, made up of members who are executives in the energy industry (BHEF, 2013). The advisory board identified the high-demand fields, engaged high-level industry support, demonstrated early successes, and used the university to target intervention through education (BHEF, 2013).

The success of the energy industry partnership at UH was attributed to the effective advisory board. The members identified actual workforce realities, based on identifying demand for specific workforce skills in an industry requiring a high skill level. With the help of the advisory committee, UH administrators analyzed and determined their earlier petroleum-engineering program to be unsuccessful because it operated in isolation, focusing only on academics instead of including business and industry input. The problem with omitting business and industry was lack of connection to current changes and trends in the industry; no internships or scholarships; and no student-industry connections leading to future employment. At the outset, the advisory board was informal and consisted of volunteers, but enthusiasm quickly grew to create motivation within the community. Members were recruited through networking and business connections, sharing their opinions and expertise. The oil and gas industry prides itself on being represented by the top minds in the country, willing to share their ideas and money to invest in new technologies and their future. Industry personnel were interested in joining the committee and contributing financially, with the realization that this effort would result in replenishing a well-trained employee pool to replace retiring engineers. A factor in enticing executives to contribute financially was an expectation of a return on their investment, in the form of future employees receiving practical knowledge. The interest of other community businesses in a continual supply of specifically trained employees was also a contributing factor that helped advisory members and other businesses invest financially. This interest sparked other industry and community support through scholarships and financial support, essential to program startup expenses and overall success. Internships helped students match their abilities with particular job skills, connect with a future employer, and establish a professional mentor in the industry. For the employer, the program provided a constant pipeline of a field-tested and industry-led specifically trained workforce (BHEF, 2013). It was not an accident that the program was a success. UH explained that this was the right program, at the right time, and in the right city (BHEF, 2013). The industry partnership involvement included members with a sincere and constant commitment to the program's development. The industry members provided invaluable availability of information sharing and development of technology (BHEF, 2013). Since education and business characteristically move at different paces, continuing to keep business and industry engaged called for communicating any advances within the community network.

Massachusetts offers one example of a higher-education advisory committee. The Board of the Massachusetts Department of Higher Education (MDHE) noted a growing need for technology innovation and IT. Research disclosed the IT workforce had grown by 36% from 2002 to 2012, and was expected to continuing growing. A shortage in technology and IT workers became evident in a continually recurring job-vacancy situation. The Board created an advisory committee, including campus representatives and industry employers, to create a strategic plan for addressing the workforce needs in the technology and IT sector (MDHE, 2014). The advisory committee was founded to address and align educational needs with training programs, to provide high-quality careers in IT and technology for future employment growth, and to supply training to match the changing market demand. In 2012, the MDHE had created a workforce plan to address the healthcare nursing shortage. This focused on educating 66% of nurses at the baccalaureate level or higher by 2020, creating a "2-4" national transfer agreement in which the nursing program participated. (The "2-4" transfer agreement is known as an articulation agreement, referring to a partnership between colleges and four-year universities wherein students move seamlessly from one institution to another) Massachusetts is one of nine states to align the curriculum to addressing the shortage (MDHE, 2014). The MDHE created the advisory committee to assist with the goal of suggesting a strategic workforce plan to the Board within one year, similar to what had been accomplished previously with the nursing program.

Many companies are looking for employees with critical thinking, communication, and problem-solving skills received through their higher-education training. The ever-changing field of technology is impacting areas of employment that require education and training in information technology. This emergence of required technical skills in the job force characterizes many fields, but especially the healthcare sector. Healthcare providers are using data and patient records to more effectively manage their patients. Technology skills are required of all healthcare workers at all levels, especially in areas where none was previously required. Degree programs are being revamped to include access to courses that were traditionally not required by the general health sector, as well as in other job areas (MDHE, 2014). The following in-demand middle-skill IT careers require a two-year education: computer systems analyst, medical and health information technicians, web developers, and data clusters. Jobs in demand requiring a four-year degree in higher education programs include: computer science, information technology, information systems, software engineering, and digital science (MDHE, 2014). In many states, the department of education will appoint an advisory committee made up of industry leaders, critical partners, faculty, and administrators, to form a joint task force to explore a strategic plan to train, partner, and provide internships and employment in the healthcare field (MDHE, 2014).

The previous research shows advisory committees are diverse in nature and institutions are using them in a variety of ways. The University of Mississippi (UM) just recently used one of their many advisory committees for a specific use to satisfy community concerns. The UM used their advisory committee to assist the Chancellor in renaming an administrative building in response to an issue of political correctness regarding the name on the building (Korn, 2017). The committee was called together for one specific purpose to recommend to the Chancellor a new name to acknowledge the history of the school without offending citizens within the community (Korn, 2017). This is just another example of the flexibility and scope an advisory committee can be called upon for recommendations. The University of Mississippi Medical Center (UMMC) also has internal and external medical advisory committees made-up of renowned researchers and scientists with various interest who assess and review future direction of the medical center for UM (UMMC, 2017). The university is taking advantage of their prestigious faculty members as well as specialists within the community and are placing them on advisory committees that meet their expertise.

CONCLUSION

One challenge for a successful advisory committee is deciding whom to place on the committee, and how they will become successful. An example of how to answer these questions is in the successful partnership with the University of Houston, which demonstrated how business and industry working collaboratively with education could successfully address regional workforce challenges. The advisory board purposely linked business and higher education experts together, to build a global program. To maximize the impact and create sustainable participation by members from business/industry and higher education, effective independent leaders were aligned to work collaboratively together as one leadership committee. Each executive used leadership skills to:

- Transfer to the community the message of what meeting the demands of the 21st century workforce would entail
- Solicit peer support for undergraduate workforce goals
- Ask for development of corporate policies to align with the goals of education and workforce needs (BHEF, 2013).

Asking businesses to align their policy to that of education and the demands of the workforce requires goal-oriented individuals to become advocates for their company's investment in the strategic educational goals. These individuals include intellectual experts in business and industry, dedicated to collaborating with higher education to create internships, programs, and courses. Other communities and various projects can utilize the BHEF findings, experiences, and lessons (2013).

The field of higher education is experiencing changes and demands brought about by society and greater legislative expectations. The changes in expectations, values, training, curriculum, outcomes, funding, and new advances are transforming higher education. Too often, and as a recurring situation, colleges are receiving decreased revenues granted to higher education by the states, despite enrollment growth and continued inflation of operating expenses. How the higher-education administration reacts to those decisions has a direct impact on the college's entire district. Students should not be shortchanged when it comes to their education, because this education equates to skilled workers to fill jobs in the workforce. Colleges and universities must remain accessible and affordable, but at the same time run efficiently and keep abreast of changes in the marketplace.

REFERENCES

Abbott, S. (2014). Hidden curriculum. *The glossary of education reform.* Retrieved from http://edglossary.org/hidden-curriculum

ACT. (2012). Preparing community college students for jobs and careers. Washington, D.C. Retrieved from http://act.rg/research/policymakers/pdf/changing_lives.pdf

ACT. (2016). Job profiling. Washington, D.C. Retrieved from http://www.act.org/content/ act/en/products-and-services/workforce-solutions/act-workkeys/job-profiling.html

American Association of Community Colleges and National Center on Education and the Economy. (2009). *Sustaining Partnerships for Regional Economic Growth.*

Baber, A. (2011). Using community colleges to build a STEM-skilled workforce. *NGA Center for Best Practices*. Retrieved from http://www.nga.org/cms/home/nga-center-for-best-practices/center-publications/page-edu-publications/col2-content/main-content-list/using-community-colleges-to-buil.html

Beach, A., Henderson, C., & Finkelstein, N. (2011). Facilitating change in undergraduate STEM instructional practices: An analytic review of the literature. *Journal of Research in Science Teaching*, *48*(8), 952–984. doi:10.1002/tea.20439

Blum, J. (2016, December 24). Oil rig jobs might soon fall to technology. *Midland Reporter Telegram, pp. 1A, 6A.*

Business and Higher Education Forum. (2013). Forging Strategic Business Partnerships to Develop the 21st Century Workforce: A Case Study of the University of Houston's Undergraduate Petroleum Engineering Program. Retrieved from https://eric.ed.gov/?q=+biomedical+workforce+advisory+committees&ft=on&ff1=dtySince_2013&id=ED559641/

Carlson, P., Holm, R., & Uvalde, R. (2011). Building regional partnerships for economic growth and opportunity. *Jobs for the Future*. Retrieved from http://futureworks-web.com/pdfs/Building_Regional_Partnerships.pdf

Carson, (2011). A meta-analysis of different forms of shared leadership-team performance relations. Retrieved from http://jom.sagepub.com/content/early/2014/03/06/0149206314525205

Cohen, A., & Brawer, F. (2008). *The American community college*. San Francisco, CA: Jossey-Bass, Inc.

Cohen, A., Brawer, F. B., & Kisker, C. B. (2013). *The American community college*. San Francisco, CA: Jossey-Bass, Inc.

Cronen, S., & Murphy, C. (2013) Participation in noncredit and occupational training and education. American Institute for Research. Retrieved from https://nces.ed.gov/surveys/gemena/pdf/NoncreditPaper_AIR_Final508.pdf

Day, M. (2001). Faculty perceptions of advisory committee effectiveness at two-year technical college. *Journal of Education for Business*, *110*(2), 194–198.

Destefano, D. (2011). Khalifa Bin Zayed Al Nahyan Foundation Provides MD Anderson with $150 Million Grant Retrieved from https://www.mdanderson.org/publications/conquest/fall-2011/khalifa-bin-zayed-al-nahyan-foundation.html

Gonzalez-Rivera, C. (2016). Building the workforce of the future. *Center for an urban future.* Retrieved from http://files.eric.ed.gov/fulltext/ED567868.pdf

Greenstone, M., & Looney, A. (2011). *Building America's job skills with effective workforce programs: A training strategy to raise wages and increase work opportunities.* The Hamilton Project. Retrieved from http://www.brookings.edu/~/media/research/files/papers/2011/11/training%20greenstone%20looney/11_training_greenstone_looney.pdf

Guidelines for Instructional Programs in Workforce Education. (2015). Guidelines for instructional workforce education. Texas Higher Education Coordinating Board.

Hamilton, V. (2004). *Building communities with a competitive workforce advantage. Sustaining Partnerships for Regional Economic Growth* (pp. 30–34). Washington, D.C.: American Association of Community Colleges.

Haralson, L. (2010). What is workforce development? *Federal Reserve Bank of St. Lewis.* Retrieved from https://www.stlouisfed.org/Publications/Bridges/Spring-2010/What-is-Workforce-Development#fn1

Heitman, E. (2005). Ivey Tech forms new workforce development department. *Community College Week, 18*(6), 17.

Hodges, R. (2012). *The road half traveled.* East Lansing, MI: Michigan State University Press.

Holzer, H. J. (2008). Workforce training: What works? Who benefits? Retrieved from http://www.familyimpactseminars.org/s_wifis28c02.pdf

Hughes, B. (2016). Worldwide Contributions. Retrieved from https://www.bakerhughes.com /company/corporate-social-responsibility/people-and-society/community-engagement/worldwide-contributions

Jacobs, R. (2007). Emergence of Workforce Development. Retrieved from www.economicmodeling.com/resources/wp-content/uploads/2007/11/jacobs_hawley-emergenceofworkforcedevelopment.pdf

Kazis, R. (2011). *Brookings-Rockefeller Project on state metropolitan innovation*. Washington, D.C.: Jobs for the Future.

Kilcrease, K. M. (2011). Faculty perceptions of business advisory boards: The challenge for effective communication. *Journal of Education for Business*, *86*(2), 78–83. doi:10.1080/08832323.2010.480989

Korn, M. (19 December 2016). *College enrollment slumps*. Wall Street Journal. p. A3.

Lane Community College. (2013). *CAHM Successful Committee Presentation*. Retrieved from http://www.lanecc.edu/ctecc/advisory-committees

LaRose, C. (2014). Workforce development in America: A brief history. Retrieved from https://www.linkedin.com/pulse/20141015154244-57121104-workforce-development-in-america-a-brief-history/

Library of Congress. (2010). Education and the workforce committee. Retrieved from https://www.congress.gov/committee/house-education-and-the-workforce/hsed0

Massachusetts Department of Higher Education. (2014). Technology talent initiative workforce plan. *The Vision Project*. Retrieved from http://www.mass.edu/bhe/lib/reports/2014-05-05DHETechnologyWorkforcePlan.pdf

McEwen, M. (2016, December 17). Unemployment falls for 2nd straight month. *Midland Reporter Telegram.*, *1A*, 4A.

National Center for Education and the Economy. (2009). Community college advisory panel. Retrieved from https://professionals.collegeboard.org/higher-ed/community-colleges/advisory-panel

National Center for Education Statistics. (2010). *Career/Technical Education (CTE) Statistics*. (Table P108). Retrieved from http://nces.ed.gov/surveys/ctes/tables/P108.asp

National Center for Education Statistics. (2012). *Higher education: Gaps in access and persistence study*. Retrieved from http://nces.ed.gov/pubs2012/2012046/index.asp

National Center for Education Statistics. (2012). U.S. Background Information Prepared for the OECD Postsecondary Vocational Education and Training "Skills Beyond School" Study. Retrieved from http://nces.ed.gov/surveys/ctes/pdf/Postsec VET.pdf

Northouse, P. G. (2013). *Leadership: Theory and practice*. Los Angeles, CA: Sage Publishing.

Pelletier, S. G. (2012). High-performing committees: What makes them work? Retrieved from https://www.agb.org/trusteeship/2012/5/high-performing-committees-what-makes-them-work

Perna, L. (2012). *Preparing today's students for tomorrow's jobs in metropolitan America*. Philadelphia, PA: University of Pennsylvania Press.

Prevention and Control of Influenza with Vaccines (PCIV): Recommendations of the advisory committee on immunizations practices, United States. (2015-2016). Influenza Season. *American Journal of Transplantation*, 15(10), 2767–2775. doi:10.1111/ajt.13505 PMID:26382204

Schaeffer, D., & Rouse, D. (2014). Effective academic advisory committee relationships. *Contemporary issues in education research*. Retrieved from http://files.eric.ed.gov/fulltext/EJ1073283.pdf

Soares, L. *The power of the education-industry partnership*. Retrieved from http://americanprogress.org/issues/labor/report/2010/10/04/8518/thepoweroftheeducation

Stevens, L. (2016). Amazon gets on jobs bandwagon. *The Wall Street Journal*, January 13. B1/B4.

Texas Higher Education Coordinating Board. (2014). *Advisory Boards*. Retrieved from http://www.thecb.state.tx.us/index.cfm?objectid=8C1EF7E7-A71E-47E6-53FE5EFA82F3880C

Texas State Library. (2016). Texas historical records advisory board. Retrieved from https://www.tsl.texas.gov/thrab

The University of Mississippi. (2017). Advisory Committees. Retrieved from https://www2.umc.edu/Administration/Centers_and_Institutes/Mississippi_Center_for_Clinical_and_Translational_Research/External_Advisory_Committee.aspx

Vocational Education Act, 1963. Public Law 88-210o Part A. Retrieved from http://cte.unt.edu/about/cte-history-of-legislation

Wethe, D. (2017). Drilling is back. What about the workers? *Bloomberg Businessweek.*, *30*(January), 14–15.

Workforce Development Overview. (2012). Employment & career development. *Employment Security Department.* Retrieved from http://www.wa.gov/esd/training/elearning/business/01-01.pdf

World Economic Forum. (2016). Future workforce strategies. Retrieved from http://reports. weforum.org/future-of-jobs-2016/future-workforce-strategy/ http://reports.weforum.org/future-of-jobs-2016/future-workforce-strategy/

ADDITIONAL READING

Ecodev (2013). Workforce. Retrieved from http://www.sugarlandecodev.com/Data-Center-Workforce---Data-Center.aspx

Engberg, M. (2007). Educating the workforce for the 21st century: A cross-disciplinary analysis of the impact of the undergraduate experience on students development of a pluralistic orientation. *Research in Higher Education*, *48*(3), 283–317. doi:10.1007/s11162-006-9027-2

Gellner, R. (2013). Obama unveils plan to make college education more affordable. Retrieved from http://www.examiner.com/article/obama-unveils-plan-to-make-college-education-more-affordable

Gonzalez, J. (2012). Multiple factors fuel growth in transfers to 2-year colleges. *The Chronicle of Higher Education.* Retrieved from http://chronicle.com/article/Multiple-Factors-Fuel-Growth/130978/

Price, D. V., & Roberts, B. (2009). *Improving student success by strengthening developmental education in colleges: The role of state policy.* The Working Poor Families Project. Retrieved from http://www.workingpoorfamilies.org/pdfs/WPFP_policybrief_winter08-09.pdf

U.S. Department of Education. (2012). *Workforce.* Retrieved from http://www.ed.gov

KEY TERMS AND DEFINITIONS

Seamless Transition: Establishing a high level of interagency collaboration that is an effective way to ensure that students transfer from high schools to post-secondary educational institutions.

Stakeholder: Anyone having an interest in a project, such as investors, employees, customers, suppliers, students, administrators, faculty, businesses, industry, and individuals.

Sustainable Economic Development: Measures the country's well-being and how well a country is performing to improve or sustain the dimensions of development, based on data.

Vocational Education: Educational training that provides practical experience in an occupational field.

Work-Study Program: Students working part-time on or off campus while enrolled in program courses, to help offset cost of courses and gain real-world experiences in a field of interest.

Chapter 2 The Roles and Characteristics of Advisory Committees

Julie Neal
Independent Researcher, USA

ABSTRACT

The advisory committee represents the institution, as the voice of the department, utilizing effective practices and strategies in decision-making. Because workforce education is technical and complex in nature, experienced and knowledgeable industry-based individuals are needed to advise, guide, and make decisions to achieve optimum outcomes. Key individuals have the ability to influence a group to achieve a common goal. The members have established respect and trust among the stakeholders, and are better prepared to handle the leadership roles and achieve results for the committee. The committee focuses on equal representation and balance; decision-making process; and acting as the voice of the project. This chapter focuses on the role of advisory committees. The chapter will also concentrate on the characteristics that comprise an advisory committee, and address identifying the most effective members to include on a committee.

INTRODUCTION

Community-college workforce-education programs, in collaboration with local businesses and industries, offer specific training opportunities to guide students toward a career path leading to employment. Workforce and technical programs offer easy access to programs, quick return on educational

DOI: 10.4018/978-1-5225-4083-0.ch002

investment, and means of encountering a variety of career and educational interests (Holzer, 2008). By definition, technical programs offer both academic and career-oriented courses, providing students with the opportunity to gain work experience through internships, job shadowing, on-the-job training, and industry-certification opportunities (Abbott, 2014). Workforce development is the coordination of public and private sector policies and programs that provide individuals with the opportunity to work for a sustainable income (Jacobs & Hawley, 2007). By enrolling in a local community college to gain new skills or retrain for emerging technologies, students may expedite achieving their full potential as an active member of society.

Advisory committees are a requirement for all educational workforce programs, as described in the Guidelines for Instruction Programs in Workforce Education (GIPWE, 2015). They are instrumental in providing funding, job placement, training, management, equipment, and support. Because the development and operation of workforce programs is complex in nature, the Texas Higher Education Coordinating Board (THECB) requires each community-college workforce-education program to implement and document an industry-based advisory committee. Advisory-committee members are typically selected for a two-to-three-year term, and voluntarily serve as consultants (Lane Community College [LCC], 2013). In Texas community colleges, advisory-committee members typically serve two-year terms, and may be reappointed (GIPWE, 2015). A variety of considerations influence member selection, including relevant expertise, experience, willingness to serve, and recommendations from other advisory members (GIPWE, 2015). Additionally, advisory-committee members also function as links between colleges and businesses, helping to facilitate internships and other opportunities for students (Day, 2001).

Advisory committees serve as a bridge between community colleges and business/industry, helping to develop a rapport with professionals in industry to assist community colleges with future programs and support (Day, 2001; Kilcrease, 2011). Advisory committees represent the stakeholders at specific campuses, by providing recommendations to college administrators regarding the education and training needs of the community, best practices available to meet those needs, requirements of specific programs, adding or removing programs, and advice for addressing differences between advisory members (GIPWE, 2015). The committee informs college leadership, specifically relating to workforce-education, grants, and business/industry training (GIPWE, 2015). Further, the advisory committee assists the college in preparing recommended customized training programs to fit within a specific budget, and within the requirements of the college and business partners (THECB, 2013).

As noted, an advisory committee guides and counsels college leaders and stakeholders on the best course of action for prospective and existing programs (GIPWE, 2015). The guidelines establish specific program requirements, the uses of an advisory committee and its functions and composition, and specifics for meeting minutes (GIPWE, 2015). Nonetheless, not only the field of education, but also business/industry and the medical field use advisory committees, to be discussed in later chapters.

Advisory committees basically exist to advise educators and/or business and industry on the design, development, implementation, evaluation, maintenance, and revision of technical/occupational educational programs (Teitel, 1994). Each advisory committee is made up of individuals with experience and expertise in the occupational field that the program serves. The advisory committee does not have any legal authority for the organization or the program; its function is to provide assistance, advise, and make recommendations (Caparosa, 1984). The committees also promote the programs in the community, and offer suggestions on ways to improve the program or update it to make modern advancements. Research indicates that the long-term successful partnership between an advisory committee and an academic unit will result in members seeing positive results. It is important to find members who are willing to commit, as well as administrative staff to organize each meeting (Rouse & Schaeffer, 2014). Active advisory committee members add credibility to programs, and promote in the local area what is happening in the committee. The professionals' input ensures programs are on the cutting edge and do not operate in a vacuum (Rouse & Schaeffer, 2014).

As for community colleges, the Texas Higher Education Coordinating Board (THECB) requires an industry-based advisory committee to supervise each workforce-education program (GIPWE, 2015). The advisory committee consists of members who are knowledgeable in workforce and technical skills, and who can provide direction for the workforce-educational programs. The committee explores and documents programmatic needs; determines adequate resources and appropriate programmatic design; suggests program revisions; evaluates designed curriculum; identifies the skills and knowledge needed to meet business/industry needs; and ensures business/industry participation (GIPWE, 2010). The workforce-education program provides certification and training run by the community college, with input from advisory committees.

The committees serve to promote effective community engagement, generate community interest, develop courses, recommend development of courses, identify business needs, secure corporate participation, and offer professional guidance to the college (Texas Workforce Commission, 2013).

Community colleges consult and work together with business/industry, forming results-driven beneficial programs to prepare students, and help the college stay informed of current advances (Hodges, 2012). The college's collaborative advisory committees guide and advise community colleges and the stakeholders regarding the best course of action regarding prospective and current programs (Carlson et al., 2011). The advisory committee consists of skilled decision-makers, key to the success of education and business partnerships (Carlson et al., 2011). Even though the advisory members do not have the authority to make formal decisions, as expert decision-makers their input is invaluable to the discussion, resulting in educated and informed recommendations to the committee.

A broad representation of the demographics of the service area characterizes advisory committees (GIPWE, 2010). While each community-college district has its own guidelines for advisory committees, they all generally consist of individuals within the community who can offer current and relevant advice, as well as generate public support for the programs. In workforce education programs, an advisory committee is industry based (GIPWE, 2010). The individuals on the advisory committee generally consist of industry leaders, such as economic-development directors, district and county judges, county commissioners, bankers, financial advisers, business leaders, the workforce dean, and local college administrators.

Advisory committees are also a pivotal part of the decision-making in business and industry. Since the state does not mandate advisory committees for business and industry, it is up to individual corporations to dictate their own meeting components. Because the decision process is more complex, due to the demand for accountability, curriculum changes, and diversity regarding stakeholders, no real guideline exists to aid the process. According to Courtney Leatherman (1998), a single individual or group can unfortunately derail or impede decisions through inaction. Any delay or indecision by the advisory committee hurts its overall effectiveness, and may cause members to drop off and leave. Proven decision-makers and leaders within their profession are vital to communication with stakeholders. It has become apparent that a gap exists in transparency regarding how administrative decisions are made and the justification to the stakeholders for these choices.

THE ROLE OF ADVISORY COMMITTEES

The World Economic Forum (2016) future of jobs report states that a lack of understanding of the disruption that changes cause business and industry requires thorough consideration. Specifically, there is a lack of alignment between what the workforce considers its strategies, and the available workers to fill in those gaps. Advisory committees can work with key individuals in the community that have firsthand experience in these areas, who can bring specific needs to the committee, and ask for recommendations from the community to implement the changes and demands a changing society requires.

More than ever, advisory committee members are combining efforts with those of business and industry leaders, forming results-driven, mutually beneficial workforce outcomes. These committee members provide dynamic relationships with business/industry in support of current workforce demands (Hodges, 2012). Key to the success of the educational and business collaboration are the combined participants' efforts through the advisory committees, and the utilization of skilled decision-making processes. As noted above, the advisory committee is the vital key provider of negotiations in developing and implementing programs, training, and curriculum in workforce and technical areas (Hodges, 2012).

An advisory committee is a select group of members in specific workforce development that provides knowledge and guidance. Advisory committees help prepare and provide expertise and experience, and influence the direction of the workforce development (GIPWE, 2015; LCC, 2013). The goal of an advisory committee is to provide expert advice on the development and continuity of workforce development, and to provide insight into relevant knowledge and skills needed in the labor force (GIPWE, 2015; Minnesota State Colleges and Universities [MNSCU], 2013). When reviewing, or proposing an educational workforce program, an advisory committee is responsible for (Figure 1) program effectiveness, curriculum planning, public relations, internships, upgrading of facilities, program elimination and expansion, and leadership (Collin Community College [CCC], 2011; LCC, 2013). Committee members are expected to offer professional advice and programmatic recommendations based on their professional experience (CCC, 2011; LCC, 2013). Advisory committees are especially helpful to

Figure 1. Responsibilities of the educational workforce program advisory committee

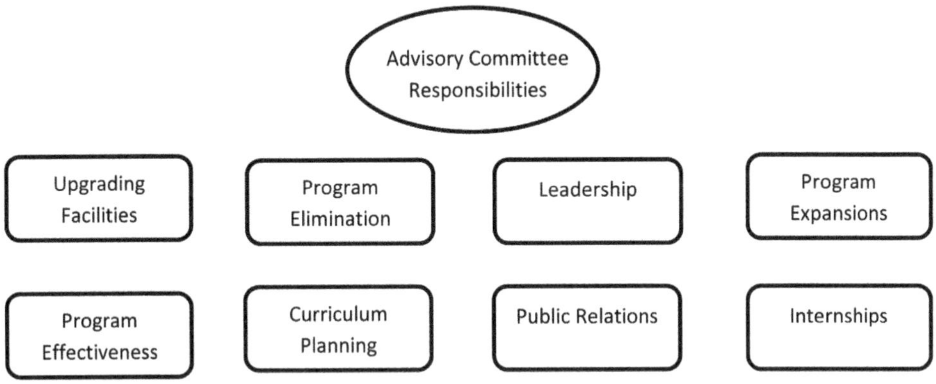

community colleges when they help create programs, obtain resources, and develop public awareness of the training programs (CCC, 2011; LCC, 2013).

Advisory committees across the county solve problems and assist business and industry in transforming to meet the needs of an ever-growing society. The idiosyncrasies of each advisory committee may be unique to its area; yet, especially in medical, technical, business, and industrial fields, they are certain to be found. More specifically, the Economic Development Program Advisory Committee (EDPAC) (2016) in California uses advisory committees known as Workforce & Economic Performance Advisory Committees (WEDPAC), to focus on advising to meet the needs for filling jobs, and match the economy's newest demands. California's advisory members include: policy advocate, technical assistant, instructors, business managers, energy, construction, utilities, community college senate and deans, business officers, trustees, K-12 policy director, workforce director, and student services officer (USDL, 2016). These are a few of the major members of the advisory committee representing California, similar to advisory committees across the nation, consisting of a balance of representatives from the community. A typical committee evolves and changes, adding members as needed to represent other areas of business and industry as they move into the community. Individuals and representatives of community organizations with expertise join, to create and give advice regarding opportunities for competitive employment (USDL, 2016). Whether the program is medical or part of business/industry, relevant and knowledgeable individuals working in the field and sharing their expertise work together to accomplish one goal, leading to the success of any advisory committee.

The typical advisory committee serves as primary means of providing input regarding the development, strategies, policies, and activities of workforce, and business/industry programs (Federal Contractors Association [FCA], 2017). Interested individuals have the ability to influence the direction of the committee for the greater good of the entire program. Experienced, goal-oriented members use their voice to enhance training, share retention ideas, and explain best practices to the committee, demonstrating their investment in the industry (FCA, 2017).

GENERAL ADVISORY COMMITTEE CHARACTERISTICS

Advisory committees have increased nationally, to create a competitive advantage and utilize their members' experiences in business to discuss strategy and planning in specific workforce and medical programs (Day, 2001; Kilcrease, 2011). Kilcrease (2011) reports the most successful advisory boards use two-way communication, including the board members and faculty, with the greatest contributions in the areas of fundraising, current marketing trends, curriculum development, and accreditation requirements (Kilcrease, 2011).

The advisory committee is important to the workforce education program, functioning as the liaison for businesses, community, stakeholders, and colleges (Harrison, 1975). Typically, meetings are held in offices or businesses; however, productive advisory committees may get together where members feel comfortable and at ease sharing their ideas. The most successful advisory committees meet in shops, in the field, at labs, or at business locations, instead of in a formal classroom or meeting area (Day, 2001). Day (2001) also reports more success when advisory members represent various specialties, occupations, and expertise (Day, 2001). The collective unique experiences of the advisory-committee members have the ability to shape and provide valuable information for project/program success. Therefore, including a diverse group of experts on the committee will provide a complete, and even a competitive perspective. It is a difficult task to unify a diverse group of individuals, but since no matter what the project/program is, the advisory-committee members are instrumental in finding and securing funding, facility instructor resources, advice, and ideas for projects and/or programs, and unity is fundamental to overall success. Including business and industry leaders that have firsthand knowledge of the skills that are active and in demand keeps the committee relevant. Advisory committees can facilitate internships for students, raise funds for programs, provide speakers and faculty, and help individuals to locate gainful employment (Riendeau, 1967; Teitel, 1994). To be effective, the committee serves to suggest changes and updates to keep the program current and applicable to society (Kerka, 2002).

The advisory committee exists for the duration of the workforce or technical program. An advisory committee spearheads the decision-making process, engaging in the process from inception, and continues to be active and fluidly participate in the programs until they cease to exist (AACC & NCEE, 2009; Kazis, 2011). The role of the committee is ongoing and active throughout the duration of the program (Kerka, 2002). The purpose of the advisory committee is to use result-driven practices to improve the prosperity of businesses (AACC & NCEE, 2009; Kerka, 2002), streamline areas in need, and integrate new ideas into programs. Even though working collaboratively to make informed decisions in workforce development is challenging, the implications will be worth the time. It is beneficial to all parties that they give the committee the freedom to seek out alliances with participants to work collaboratively to make informed decisions. The decision-making process utilized by the advisory committee and the researcher must be collaborative and dependent upon one another.

An effective advisory committee needs proven leaders and guidelines that will require modifications to adjust for changing conditions and environments. A workforce-education advisory committee is effective when it includes practical working members serving the needs of the community, as well as the business and industry they serve (Barbee, 2005). New career advances are constantly changing. As new technology emerges and makes its way into business and industry, the advisory committee is the link that keeps department chairs, managers, and institutions well informed of the changes and tends. They also are skilled in advising how and where to concentrate on those skills that will be in demand. Since business and industry personnel have a direct connection to the community, they are also the link to training and education. Within the educational system, the advisory committee does not have administrative authority, nor can it establish policy. Therefore, it takes a strong member to support and put forth the effort, all the while realizing the administration can exercise authority over any decisions the committee makes. The basic advisory committee functions similarly to advisory committees found all across the country. Each program and its membership are unique because of the diverse member backgrounds and knowledge they bring to the committee; however, they all function in basically the same way, grounded in the overall characteristics of advisory committees across the county, as this example based on the Nevada Department of Education protocol:

1. Establish a need and understanding.
2. Develop a quality program.
3. Each member should have equal voice.
4. Membership should be representative of the community.
5. Include local, successful, interested, and practical members.
6. Committee should be willing to make allowances in time and delivery of meetings to accommodate all members — via email, teleconferences, Internet feeds, webcasts, etc.
7. Committee is advisory only — no administrative or policy power.
8. Committee assists in upgrading equipment, providing instructors, identifying current standards, and identifying members who are willing to publicly addresses the community on behalf of the advisory committee (Barbee, 2005).

The basic committee can operate with formal or informal rules; however, a strong leader who can keep meetings organized and on task should be at the helm. Some committees find it useful to rotate leaders according to the meeting agenda. This helps generate a shared interest and ownership among the committee members. The overall goal of the committee is to provide leadership, guidance, technical assistance, improvement, further development, and even internships and donations (Barbee, 2005).

WHO SHOULD BE INCLUDED ON THE COMMITTEE?

The committee can include local business/industry leaders, owners, and managers; community members who want the community to grow; those individuals that truly have heart for a project; a chamber of commerce director; former students; field managers; office personnel; local judges; or county commissioners. Membership of the committee is basically the call of the department chair, with recommendations from those already on the committee. Choosing the right members is one of the most important and effective steps in promoting the success of the committee. Since the advisory committee is pivotal to providing funding, equipment, support, advice, and personal support, it is more important than ever to select individuals who want the program to succeed, and have a commitment to help. A collaborative relationship among the participants working with the advisory committee will have an effect on the outcome of the program; therefore, individuals that know how to communicate and have a strong network within the community are beneficial to developing committee rapport. Because the members will have to justify their input to the stakeholders, someone with communication skills would benefit the committee in soliciting community support. Advisory committee members face challenges as part of the decision-making process, as they come to agreements and justify their rationale for the decisions, to one another and to the stakeholders. A member who is willing to become a champion for the entire committee, with communication skills and overall knowledge of the project, is valuable to helping gain the support of the stakeholders.

Including top-level managers and executives who have worked their way up the ranks adds credibility to the advising process. Individuals that have experienced making difficult decisions, and understand the entire process from all levels, have vital knowledge to share with the committee. Including business/industry individuals with a history of working together with respect, trust, discretion, and confidentiality is wise. Members who convey their message and communicate with each member on the committee, so that all members grasp the concepts being shared, are also helpful. A committee member who runs a value-driven company, and acts as a negotiator for the company to maximize return on investment, will also be likely to take the same initiative with advice to the advisory committee. Melding business philosophy with that of education makes for sound decisions. It is important to the committee's success to include local individuals proven in business/industry. Reputation in the community will likely precede the individual on the committee. A member who is opportunity driven and a solution provider will likely use this same process in helping the advisory committee reach its own solutions and decisions. Program expectations are becoming more complex and difficult, with demands created by adjustments to change, technology, and the challenges of meeting program requirements. Adding or adjusting a program to fit program requirements can be challenging and expensive. Utilizing the knowledge and advice of local proven executives and managers, who understand the culture and clientele of the business, will help a program be successful. Including business and industry members with years of experience and a proven track record can make the difference between a quality committee and one that just exists.

Utilizing local business and industry managers, CEOs, and presidents can create checks and balances for advisory committees, between education and workforce. Administrators in business/industry deal with workforce changes and challenges, which can occur locally, across states, and even globally. Seeking out the recommendations and knowledge of local leaders can help the advisory committee realize whether adding, updating, or eliminating programs will be an economically sound decision for the institution. The training the system produces for the student must be marketable within the society for many years, and a draw for other students seeking similar skills. Business and industry leaders have their ear to the market, listening to the wants and needs of the workforce. By including these talented individuals on the advisory committee, the committee has current and relevant information on trends and changes in the workforce. The committee will also learn to use business techniques to compete and operate in a challenging workforce environment.

There can be negative aspects to having outside members on the advisory committee. If a board or committee becomes ineffective, and the members are just there because they must be, the committee may need restructuring and revitalization. Whether it is an advisory board or a committee, the members need to participate and be active members for efficiency and program growth. Enlisting the right people, with the knowledge and subject-matter expertise to ask the right questions, is key; otherwise, the committee will be unable to achieve its goals. Having the right people on the committee follows the adage that the leader is only as good as the team of people around him or her (Holtschneider, 2013). Knowing whom to ask and how to ask pertinent questions is paramount to the effectiveness of the committee, which suggests recruiting members who are linked, and have a deep connection to community industries and extensive knowledge regarding operating complexities (Holtschneider, 2013). This is true on the institution's behalf as well, including administrators with accreditation and standards knowledge to keep the committee on the right track within their scope of authority, and not waste time going in improbable directions. The committee should never feel an outcome has been predetermined, which leads to everyone's frustration. Each member must know that time and appearance at the meetings are valuable, and that insight and input is key to the group's success. Carlson et al. (2011) explain that bringing community leaders together under a general purpose prohibits a partner from having too much control. Also needed is a well-planned and thought-out meeting prior to inception, with an agenda guiding the main course of actions, describing exactly why and for what purpose the members are meeting. Many institutions now set up a link for members to access additional information to look over prior to convening, as well as to keep in contact through periodic emails. Including links to members' company websites helps members become familiar with those they will engage in discussions.

An active and engaged committee is one that is proud of its efforts and has confidence that its work matters. Every member should be included and engaged in an activity, assigned to a specific task, or even to subgroups, if creating an atmosphere of competition within the committee is advisable (Holtschneider, 2013). Each member should have an opportunity to lead the committee and share his or her individual expertise with the group, creating ownership within the committee and its dedication to the program. Importantly, as each member joins the committee, make sure all members know exactly the reason for the member being asked to join the committee, which will increase the sense of usefulness, inclusion in the group, and contribution value of the member's expertise (Holtschneider, 2013).

The advisory committee's relationship with its members may be unique to each particular committee, because of the members' level of commitment. Many members are providing financial assistance to the program with equipment and monetary donations. Business and industry will also provide partnerships in the form of internships for students. As a result, the members have a substantial investment in the program, and soliciting and seeking out their knowledge and decision-making skills represent a high level of alliance. Unfortunately, not all committees and communities are fortunate enough to have the same level of commitment from their members. It takes strong leadership and community ties to achieve a complete, cohesive union of dedicated business and industry personnel, to achieve the most successful advisory committees.

CONCLUSION

Higher education and business/industry have realized in recent years that by working together, they can train a highly skilled workforce. Combining skills and experience from business and industry with the academic realm of educational institutions results in a mix of technically expert and innovative talent, ready for employment. These partnerships have the potential to result in higher wages and opportunities for individuals to move up the career ladder to future advancement (Soares, 2010). The advisory committee adds validity, analyses the programs, and identifies potential challenges to be addressed. Business and industry often do not understand the dynamics of educational institutional practices; the advisory committee can facilitate mutual understanding between the parties. The partnerships led by advisory committees result in the following best practices: workplace-based learning, support for students, accelerated degree completion, tracking student progress, designing new curriculum, shared facilities, additional resources, and simplifying enrollment for non-traditional students (Soares, 2010).

Advisory committees are the connection that binds workforce educational programs with business and industry. In the fast-paced workforce, community colleges are well adapted to making changes, but the affiliation of advisory committee members will help lead to successful program and students.

Independently, educational institutions and organizations in business and industry may be talented in their areas, but by combining efforts, they provide a unique opportunity for the students, community, and workforce. Members immersed within business and the medical industry can help instructors stay well informed of notable industry trends. The advisory committee members can open doors for students, provide leads on possible job opportunities, give advice, and help students train for skills that are highly sought after in the community.

REFERENCES

American Association of Community Colleges and National Center on Education and the Economy. (2009). *Sustaining Partnerships for Regional Economic Growth* (pp. 20–29). Washington, D.C.: American Association of Community Colleges.

Barbee, J. R. (2005). Advisory technical skills committee. Retrieved from http://files.eric.ed.gov/fulltext/ED521978.pdf

Caparosa, C. (1984). Advisory Committees. Clute Institute. Retrieved from https://www.cluteinstitute.com/ojs/index.php/CIER/article/download/8308/8338

Carlson, P., Holm, R., & Uvalde, R. (2011). Building regional partnerships for economic growth and opportunity. *Jobs for the Future.* Retrieved from http://futureworks-web.com/pdfs/Building_Regional_Partnerships.pdf

Cohen, A., & Brawer, F. (2008). *The American community college.* San Francisco, CA: Jossey-Bass, Inc.

Cohen, A., Brawer, F. B., & Kisker, C. B. (2013). *The American community college.* San Francisco, CA: Jossey-Bass, Inc.

Collin Community College. (2016). *Advisory committee handbook.* Retrieved from http://www.cc.edu/handbook/advisory/html

Day, M. (2001). Faculty perceptions of advisory committee effectiveness at two-year technical college. *Journal of Education for Business, 110*(2), 194–198.

FCA. (2017). Advisory Committee. Retrieved from http://www.finishingcontractors.org/members-resources/advisory-committees

GIPWE. (2015). Guidelines for instructional workforce education. Texas Higher Education Coordinating Board.

Harrison, W. G. (1975). The advisory committee in the community college: An overview. Retrieved from www.ehis.ebscohost.com.lib-e2.lib.ttu.edu

Hodges, R. (2012). *The road half traveled.* East Lansing, MI: Michigan State University Press.

Holzer, H. J. (2008). Workforce training: What works? Who benefits? Retrieved from http://www.familyimpactseminars.org/s_wifis28c02.pdf

Kazis, R. (2011). *Brookings-Rockefeller Project on state metropolitan innovation.* Washington, D.C.: Jobs for the Future.

Kerka, S. (2002). *Effective advisory committees.* (ERIC Information Analyses ED463411). Retrieved from ehis.ebscohost.com.lib-e2.lib.ttu.edu

Kilcrease, K. M. (2011). Faculty perceptions of business advisory boards: The challenge for effective communication. *Journal of Education for Business, 86*(2), 78–83. doi:10.1080/08832323.2010.480989

Lane Community College. (2013). *CAHM Successful Committee Presentation.* Retrieved from http://www.lanecc.edu/ctecc/advisory-committees

Leatherman, C. (1998). Report by governing-boards group urges speedier approaches to making decisions. The Chronicle of Higher Education. Retrieved from http://chronicle.com/article/Report-by-Governing-Boards/104811/

National Center for Education and the Economy. (2009). Community college advisory panel. Retrieved from https://professionals.collegeboard.org/higher-ed/community-colleges/advisory-panel

Riendeau, A. J. (1967). *The role of the advisory committee in occupational education in the junior college.* Retrieved from ehis.ebscohost.com.lib-e2.lib.ttu.edu

Schaeffer, D., & Rouse, D. (2014). Effective academic advisory committee relationships. *Contemporary issues in education research.* Retrieved from http://files.eric.ed.gov/fulltext/EJ1073283.pdf

Soares, L. (2010). The power of the education-industry partnership. Retrieved from http://americanprogress.org/issues/labor/report/2010/10/04/8518/thepoweroftheeducation

Teitel, L. (1994). *The advisory committee advantage: Creating an effective strategy for programmatic improvement.* Washington, D.C.: The George Washington University.

Texas Higher Education Coordinating Board. (2014). *Advisory Boards.* Retrieved from http://www.thecb.state.tx.us/index.cfm?objectid=8C1EF7E7-A71E-47E6-53FE5EFA82F3880C

US Department of Labor. (2016). Advisory committee on increasing competitive integrated employment for individuals with disabilities. Retrieved from https://www.dol.gov/odep/topics/wioa.htm

US Department of Labor. (2016). *The employment situation.* Retrieved from https://www.bls.gov/news.release/pdf/empsit.pd

ADDITIONAL READING

Worth, J., & Cheney, S. (2009). *Creating and maintaining partnerships at community colleges: Roles and expectations for college leaders. In Sustaining Partnerships for Regional Economic Growth* (pp. 47–51). Washington, DC: American Association of Community Colleges.

KEY TERMS AND DEFINITIONS

Curriculum: The aggregation of courses of study given in a school, college, or university.

Decision-Makers: The person who decides things, especially in an organization that uses a thought process of selecting a logical choice from available options.

Nontraditional Students: Students who do not attend college full-time and are not between the ages of 18 and 24 years of age.

Programmatic Design: Precise project footprints or specific design.

Chapter 3
Decision-Making

Julie Neal
Independent Researcher, USA

ABSTRACT

The demand for accountability and measurement regarding educational programs in community colleges makes the decision-making process of advisory committees more important than ever. The role of the advisory committee for educational workforce programs is changing, and becoming increasingly necessary, due to legislative actions and consistent changes in the workforce. Business, industry, and higher-education institutions are adapting programs to fit thriving regional economies, and calling upon advisory committees to make major decisions within their organizations. Perceptions of and experiences with the decision-making processes that educational practitioners and workforce advisory-committee members utilize to make informed decisions for workforce-education programs are vital to their success. This chapter reveals the best practices that business and industry use to make informed decisions, including how to utilize those practices to include educational entities.

INTRODUCTION

The decision-making process for workforce programs is complicated, due to constant changes in industry, curriculum modifications, and stakeholders (Day, 2001; Kilcrease, 2011). The complication can be reduced for educational institutions, workforce, and business and industry, as they will benefit from the shared experiences of diverse individuals suggesting specific guidelines

DOI: 10.4018/978-1-5225-4083-0.ch003

to aid an advisory committee in its decision-making. The experiences of administrators in college workforce and technical programs, as well as those of business executives, shared proven practices, recommendations, and advice for selection of the advisory members, help to guide advisory committees in the decision-making process for workforce programs.

The heart of these collaborations is the role of the advisory committees and their decision-making processes. Advisory committees use the knowledge of committee-member experts to make decisions regarding workforce-education programs. Influential members of the community make up the advisory committee, working in conjunction with the local community college to offer relevant advice and generate support (Carlson et al., 2011; Soares, 2010). Their varied expertise in specialized areas of the workforce enables them to advise the committee on key decisions, to produce needed quality programs. It must be pointed out that individuals make decisions every day while going about their daily activities. However, many decisions are simple and take little consideration; others can have overwhelming ramifications. Finding individuals to include on the advisory committee, who have a proven track record; ownership and pride with regard to their decisions; and a true sense of obligation for the commitment the committee is making, can serve the committee best.

The decision-making process that advisory committees use can also advance higher-education practice. The advisory committee provides processes and strategies that educational practitioners and members of the committee use, which they perceive to be effective in making informed decisions about workforce education programs. The decision-making process for the college workforce and technology programs involves collaboration with key individuals, as well as local business and industries, and has wide-ranging ramifications for the parties involved (Bess & Dee, 2011). These key business and industry leaders combine their skills and experiences, in efforts to produce a quality education program. Current leaders in business/industry and from the community-college workforce initiatives provide direction for the committee to use in the decision-making process, when determining what programs to expand, add, or discontinue, and how to do it. Business leaders have managers who can share their past and current experiences, to advise the workforce-education administrators on when to cut or add programs (Burke & Miller, 1999). These insights also help college leaders discover new program opportunities that would be beneficial in a particular region, and inform leaders about potential expansion or closure of existing programs. Since the advisory committee is made up of diverse business and industry personnel making decisions based on member collaboration to face unexpected challenges, an understanding of the decision-making process for both entities is beneficial to the productive outcome of the advisory committee (Burke & Miller, 1999).

Higher education is working with local businesses and industry in order to collaborate effectively on workforce training that carries over into the community (Hamilton, 2004). Advisory committees use the knowledge of respected committee-member experts to make decisions regarding workforce-education programs. The influential members of the community make up the advisory committee, working in conjunction with the local community college to offer relevant advice and generate support (Carlson et al., 2011). Their varied expertise in specialized areas of the workforce advises the committee on key decisions to produce needed quality programs. Focusing on the major factors involved in the decision, and using the skills and experiences of all the committee members, helps the committee consider alternatives and reach understanding and consensus that is best for the program. Higher education has the skill to influence modern society, especially in decision-making in the areas of business, education, politics, and medicine (Browne & Shen, 2017).

The ability to make decisions, and involvement of knowledgeable members on the advisory committee, are important components of the advisory committee, and the root of a successful collaboration. Looking at the nature of decision-making and its benefits, group decision-making can maximize the use of available expertise within an advisory committee (Day, 2001; Kilcrease, 2011). The decisions a college and a business make are complex, and the perspectives of multiple members are necessary to assess accurately the need and probable success of a workforce-education program (Allingham, 2002; Burke & Miller, 1999). Since advisory committees generally consist of a variety of individuals with varying leadership experiences and management styles, transparent communication is critical for group success (Bess & Dee, 2008).

Even though in a formal educational advisory committee, members have no formal power to make decisions, their input and experience is vital to the committee's success. The final decision is up to the administration in education, and to the president, owner, and/or CEO in business and industry. Nonetheless, the expertise at decision-making by the professionals on the committee is a major component of a successful group. Selecting the right individuals to serve on an advisory committee is imperative for the success of the workforce-education program. Members who have influence within the local community are instrumental in seeking support for programs, both financially and in placement of students after completion (Johnson, 2013). It is helpful if advisory committee members are enthusiastic about serving on the committee, and committed to the overall success of the program (Johnson, 2013). Their enthusiasm and leadership helps guide the committee members to agree upon decisions, and create unity among the members (Northouse, 2013). Individuals who are willing to make concessions and negotiate serve workforce-education programs best (Burke & Miller, 1999; Johnson, 2013; Northouse, 2013). Encouraging a representative from small and large independent businesses to show up and participate in meetings is important to sharing all aspects of industry needs.

Understanding the dynamics of the decision-making group is imperative for the success of the program. When a college faces complex problems to be solved, it has experts in their fields, with relevant knowledge and skills, to call upon (Bees & Dee, 2011). A group process works because of the sharing of individual ideas, all working toward a common interest, where conflict or disagreements create openness to the real issues at hand. Group decision-making helps to reveal the overall objective to the members, identifying the best course for the group to follow (Tonn, 2003). It may be necessary for the parties to engage in integrated bargaining by incorporating the party interest into the solution. The individuals involved would need to express openly their differences to all stakeholders, which in turn leads to addressing the real issues and underlying conflicts. As a result, the parties can remove any self-interest and begin negotiating for the good of the organization. In particular, advisory committees are complex entities made up of multiple talented individuals within the group. Using group decision-making utilizes all the experts together, focusing on the good of the whole, because the decision is complex and will require the perspectives of multiple experts in their fields to assess the situation accurately (Bess & Dee, 2011). Considering the perspective of several experts has been used for the success of workforce programs, leading to a direct impact on the economy and opening up future dealing with local business and industry.

In order to achieve the overall goals of the committee, Burke and Miller (1999) suggest that four discussions are necessary: the nature of the problem; possible solutions; participants who enter and leave the process; and choice opportunities (Bess & Dee, 2008; Burke & Miller, 1999). The decision-making process for education often differs from that of business and industry (Allingham, 2002; Bess & Dee, 2008; Burke & Miller, 1999). Deetz

(1992) finds that when making decisions, institutions of higher education are concerned with value and moral imperatives, as well as efficiency and effectiveness (Bess & Dee, 2008). Business and industry leaders are generally concerned with costs, return, and implementation, and operate more on result-oriented decisions, acting quickly and decisively (Carlson et al., 2011). Therefore, the two entities, using their different decision-making styles and cohesively joining ideas, can and do find unique solutions and ideas to put into practice, resulting in beneficial outcomes for both parties.

Budget, accountability to stakeholders, and justification for the decisions they are required to make drives all institutions, including businesses and colleges. The advisory members within business and industry have the ability to obtain current trends in workforce education, including modern changes and advancements. The community college's ability to collaborate with businesses and industries during the program development decision-making process facilitates future growth decisions regarding which programs to expand or negate.

Since advisory committees generally consist of a variety of individuals with varying leadership experiences and management styles (Dixon, 1990), transparent decision-making is critical for group success (Bess & Dee, 2008). Those individuals who possess skills in making accurate decisions (Jones, 2006; Spector, 2012) should be found and encouraged to join the advisory committee for the sake of its progress and success. Decision-making requires a process, whether in business or education (Jones, 2006; Spector, 2012). In order to achieve the overall goals of the advisory committee, Burke and Miller (1999) suggest that four decision-making steps are necessary (Figure 1).

These strategies can be applied to the workforce to motivate individuals to achieve a goal, and better manage team involvement (Metcalf & Urwick, 2013). The goal is to motivate managers and employers working together cooperatively, in harmony, resolving differences by finding solutions that satisfy all parties, and empowering different departments to work together on joint projects (Metcalf & Urwick, 2013; Tonn, 2003). Using managers

Figure 1. Advisory committee decision-making steps

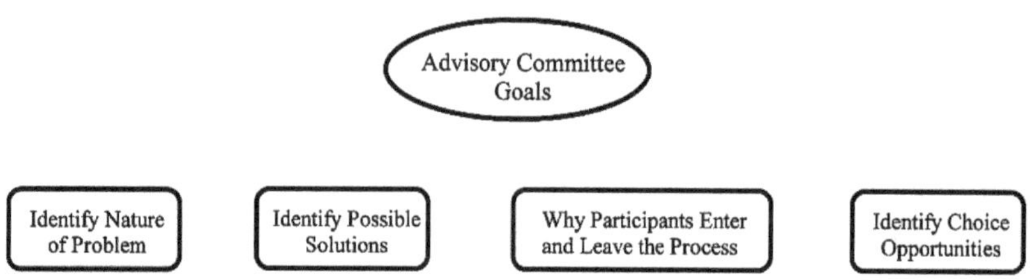

to head up the committees, while at the same time combining workers with relevant knowledge on the committee, contributes to the process (Follett, 2013; Tonn, 2003). Abandoning any competition that might create hostility and suspicion among committee members, and instead creating cooperation by taking advantage of the skills each individual committee members possesses, can promote achievement and productivity of the overall group (Follett, 2013; Metcalf & Urwick, 2013; Tonn, 2003). Management should use its knowledge in specific skills areas to influence and advise the committee toward an informed decision (Kadian-Baumeyer, 2003). This aids business and industry in deciphering if one approach is superior in structure, by obtaining and listening to experts in their fields before making final decisions. Identifying how abstract concepts have specific meaning to chief executive officers (CEO) and managers in business and industry, and how they interpret and find meaning in those scenarios, can determine whether there is similarity or a disconnect in procedures that educational administrators use. Specifically, differences and similarities between education administrators and business administrators' decision-making processes can inform how those may contribute positively or negatively to the advisory committee's logic. Business and industry rely heavily on past experiences, using measurable data (Carlson et al., 2011; Hodges, 2012). Analyzing data for an advisory committee can help determine how the advisory committee is making decisions that result in the maximum return, whether for the college, business and industry, medical organizations, or stakeholders.

ORGANIZATIONAL DECISION-MAKING

In the decision-making process, a major focus is the stakeholder, the groups or individuals directly affected by the decisions (Melé, 2006). The stakeholder puts complete trust and belief in the advisory committee, for the sake of the company. Even though social worker and political science scholar Mary Parker Follett (1918) presented the idea years ago that conflict can be instrumental in the decision-making process, studies support her work and it is important to revisit her ideas. Follett (1940) reports that it is imperative to maintain relationships with different interest groups, including consumers, investors, workers, and industry (Melé, 2006). The advisory committee must find a way to integrate and balance the interests of these stakeholders in the decision-making process. Follett's (1940) organizational approach proposes balancing the interests of stakeholders, contending that using compromise and integrated solutions satisfies both parties without either side sacrificing its needs (Melé, 2006). Follett's theory has been used to assist in the development of local community organizations, and negotiating compromises in the decision-making process in education, as well as in business studies (Smith, 2002). Widely accepted in the business community for her management approach, Follett forgoes the hierarchical structure in organizations, and opts for group contributions, in order to achieve result-driven compromises (Smith, 2002). Follett's (1940) theory can be applied to the college decision-making process, as the college fosters a culture of real services to benefit society (Melé, 2006). Including those individuals personally invested in the success of the program on the advisory committee will be conducive to negotiations, and drive the process toward achieving successful results. Solving conflicts of interest with stakeholders, by using the management technique of integration, results in a cohesive blending of ideas.

Managers within organizations make decisions daily, using a rational process based on previous experiences. However, organizations' decisions involve several multilevel individuals from various departments, viewpoints, and levels of authority, all working together. Therefore, adding to the committee a variety of members representing various administrative levels will offer a more well-rounded view from several perspectives. All of the aforementioned scenarios also apply to the college advisory committees.

EQUAL REPRESENTATION AND BALANCE

Advisory committee members have a direct connection to the economic changes within a community, an understanding of what is relevant in business and industry within the community, as well as in the industry generally. The collaborations formed with these entities represent a reciprocal relationship. Community colleges need knowledgeable, relevant, and attentive advisory members on their workforce committee, driven by the need for business and industry to work with these institutions to produce a skilled and relevant workforce (Bray, 2011; Price & Roberts, 2009). Business and industry do not have the time to train or retrain employees on their own, creating a need for the local community college to provide specialized training to help address local workforce needs.

Day (2001) and Kilcrease (2011) identify the strength of advisory committees as the wealth of knowledge they bring to workforce programs. For example, a welding presence in a community is not just the corporations that have multicomplex buildings and hire 100 welders or more. The small shops that hire less than 10 employees, but manage to keep them for the duration of their career, are a powerful resource to a community, and the advisory committee needs their representation. A well-balanced committee needs multiple perspectives to make the decisions and assess the needs of a successful workforce program (Allingham, 2002; Burke & Miller, 1999; Kilcrease, 2011). Meeting the needs of the community by offering training for critical skills needed for employment (Greenstone & Looney, 2011; Holzer, 2008) requires meeting the needs of all in the community, not just those of a select large group.

Having key business and industry leaders on the advisory committee, who have proven track records of working collaboratively with others in the community, is an asset to encouraging representation by others within the community. For example, a member with years of experience and maturity, regardless of business size, should be considered for the advisory committee. Daugherty (2015) and DiMattina (2014) note that to create a local, united community supporting the workforce-education programs, all business and industry operations, whether large corporations or small independents, must be included and provided with an avenue to share their voice. Therefore, a key element the advisory committee is diverse representation—not only with respect to ethnicities, but also diverse relative to business size and specific type within business/industry and by location. The findings of Kilcrease (2011) and Kerka (2002) identify the need to include a diverse group of business and industry personnel on the committee, to represent large and small companies.

Participation and speaking up in the advisory meeting are crucial to the overall success of the advisory committee's work. All members on the advisory committee should be encouraged to talk and share their experiences and ideas. At times, this requires a strong vocal leader for the committee, using an open and honest discussion forum without time limits, to allow anyone interested to give their input. To achieve the greatest good from the committee, practitioners suggest curtailing those with boisterous personalities from taking over the meeting. All members are encouraged to speak openly and honestly, without repercussions and with no time limits, so that all members can give their input and have time to digest the information at hand. Some members are not used to speaking in front of groups; therefore, giving all members the opportunity to feel comfortable during the meeting will encourage full participation. This requires a strong advisory committee leader, to encourage the sharing of ideas and deter those trying to control meetings and outcomes to their own advantage. Balance requires transparency, accountability, and inclusion. Advisory committee members have a direct connection to the economic changes within a community, and an understanding of what is relevant in business/industry within the community, as well as for the industry as a whole.

Combine Talents and Experiences

The members of any committee have their own experiences, training, and personal attitudes toward a project. No one individual can know everything; sharing talents and experiences creates a well-rounded and accurate analysis of the issues. The eclectic composition of the membership will guide the committee to seeing various perspectives that enable the members to reach a well-informed and concise decision for the project. The committee should solicit and encourage communication between and among members to motivate open discussions, encouraging participation from all members. The goal is for the members to share ideas and experiences in detail with one another, using suggestions and combining ideas. It is important to include on the committee members with varying opinions and from variously sized institutions, to get a well-rounded view of situations.

Building an effective leadership team that is organized, makes collective decisions, and works efficiently and effectively as a group is key to a successful advisory committee. Selected members should have experience in daily decision-making, to combat the onslaught of challenges and changes that may arise within the group; nonetheless, the team will work cohesively together to solve and share experiences in order to reach agreed upon conclusions. The committee may even need to break up into subgroups of expertise and then reemerge as one group, sharing the best solutions as agreed upon in smaller units. No one team having any more power than another, just different subject matter expertise.

Figure 2. To achieve optimal use the advisory committee uses

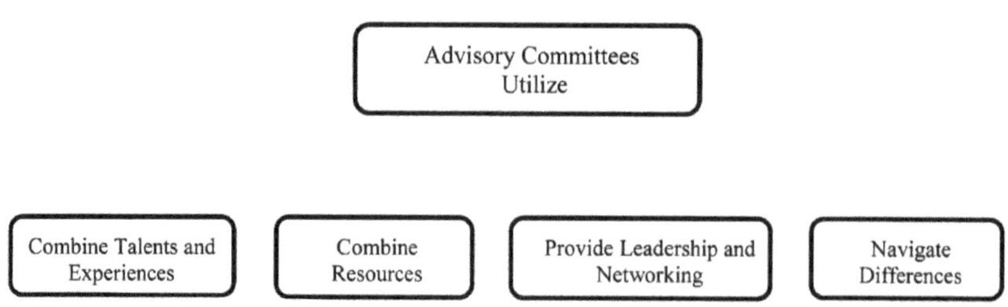

It is important that each team or group be informed fully of the task at hand to be able to share their talents and build off one another's suggestions. Developing a camaraderie between the members will encourage individuals to share their expertise and in turn build upon each other's ideas. Establishing a trust among members and a foundation of ownership will lead to the sharing of ideas and ultimately decisions the group is proud to share with administrators.

Combining Resources

Even though it is difficult to convince a leader to give up allotted funds, overall it will benefit all involved. By sharing facilities, equipment, instructors, funds, and knowledge, the committee is using all the assets at maximum utilization to train future employees. Instead of an institution buying machines or equipment that a company already has available, students could go to that facility for training, using existing equipment and the company's instructors. The funds a college may have earmarked for a program can help pay for equipment and instructors not available in the area.

Resources are not only monetary assets and equipment, but individuals and ideas from other departments and fields of study. A resource is anything that can bring assistance to the committee and make the job of the advisory committee easier and more efficient. Teams may even solicit members in the community to share ideas and be guest speakers for the group to add a different perspective to the discussions. Community colleges are known to work with tight resources and restricted budgets as well as business/industry that use the practice of lean management (McShane and Von Glinow, 2014). The management practice can help with the possible issue of limited or restricted resources as it focuses on improving efficiency and effectiveness by using lean practices (McShane and Von Glinow, 2014). Resources can be expanded by cutting down on excessive travel and inventory, down time, overloaded workers and machinery, and adapting to a changing environment (McShane and Von Glinow, 2014).

Leadership and Networking

Essential to the success of the partnership between and among members of advisory committees are the leadership and commitment of the stakeholders. Leaders who represent a local community and are familiar with the customs and idiosyncrasies of the community—having already established respect and trust among the stakeholders, and the ability to get results—are better prepared to handle leadership roles (Carlson et al., 2011). Similarly, Northouse (2013) believes that key individuals have the ability to influence a group to achieve a common goal. The leader's role in any advisory committee is not to take sole responsibility for the group, but to influence others to work toward the common goal of the committee (Carlson et al., 2011). Northouse (2013) states that a strong leader should be able to persuade people to moral responsibility that transcends their own self-interest, for the good of the entire committee.

The ability to network at meetings is a skill needed by individuals, organizations, and companies. Networking creates a sense of belonging within an environment. Social networking ties individuals and groups together (Kokkonen, 2015). Progress in technology has multiplied possibilities for networking, expanding relationships, facilitating follow-up, and making instant connections. Networking creates new business connections and channels. Communication by networking creates information sharing, relationships, and opportunities for negotiations. The key to networking is communication that includes openness, trade-offs, exchanges, and support. Members must realize what kind of information might be shared, and how the collaboration could lead to partnerships. Communication skills used while networking include reasoning, elaborating, directness, and the ability to make concessions (Kokkonen, 2015).

Navigating Differences

Communication is key during meetings, to explore and recognize members' biases, views, differences, and similarities. Building on understanding, knowledge, interaction, awareness, and sensitivity to others on the committee builds relationships and a working foundation of trust and respect within the committee. Take time to get to know the individuals on the committee, including a discussion of their successes and failures in business, and how they navigated through these periods. All members are on the committee for a reason: their knowledge and the expertise they bring to the discussion. It is important to include each member in the discussion, and help each to feel comfortable enough to share thoughts regarding the project honestly.

Including members known to have a different approach to issues helps spark discussions, and generate a new way of looking at old issues. Even if it is challenging to create rapport with these individuals, their way of seeing things helps a committee to consider all challenges they might face outside the committee. Individuals must be included on the committee who know what questions to ask, and do not hesitate to bring up the difficult questions for discussion. Including diversity within a committee can also mean diverse personalities, including individuals who look at situations from a different vantage point—for example, taking an alternative view, or seeking to find out what would happen if a committee does not act. If the committee takes no action and does not make changes, will the program be harmed in any way? Psychologists Kahneman and Tversky looked at this approach in their theory of decision-making (Lewis, 2017). The theory focused on the way questions were asked, and whether that made a difference in the outcome. Including a decision-maker on the committee, who takes a look at what the potential losses might be, as opposed to only looking at potential gains, brings enlightenment and clarity to the overall outcome of the decision (Lewis, 2017). Adding members to the committee with alternative views and opinions, as well as this unique style, might make navigating their differences difficult at the outset; however, the overall benefit will contribute value to the outcome.

HARMONY AND LEADERSHIP

The advisory committee does not want members to be put in the situation of making judgments amid uncertainty (Lewis, 2017). Choosing individuals to serve on the committee should indicate that they have experience and practice in making decisions, especially in the program they represent. In any field, whether it is medical, an oilfield, or business/industry, the decision-making of the committee members could affect great sums of money and reputations. Soliciting members with confidence, proven judgement, integrity, and fortitude will lead to sound investments in the committee's ability to recommend the right course of action. CEOs, presidents, directors, and those with decision-making authority realize and have experienced the high stakes involved in making choices, and backing up their decisions with facts for stakeholders. Having groups of individuals sharing ideas and solutions that one member alone may not be able to see is beneficial. A group of diverse individuals brings a variety of perspectives and experiences to share with the committee. Members with unusual perspectives open up possibilities for divulging data that might otherwise be overlooked, which may challenge preconceived norms (Heffernan, 2015). Utilizing a data-driven approach (Lewis, 2017), combined with expert experience in decision-making, results in higher probability of program success, instead of relying solely on one's judgment.

At the outset of creating an advisory committee, or when adding a new member, the committee may go through navigating individual differences. Experience may morph into personal bias, because the individual brings prior biases into the mix, and may see only an expected outcome (Lewis, 2017). This is why having several members on the committee with years of experience will help work through whatever prejudices and biases an individual brings along, to cultivate ownership for the project as a whole. After working together as a cohesive group, individuals will merge their ideas and decision-making skills, converting into one collective group. Each decision-maker has distinct ideas, however, and merging them requires an open atmosphere of freedom to share thoughts and ideas, without being criticized or shamed when participating. There are also pitfalls to decision-making that members need to acknowledge, in order to consider the best possible alternative, and recognize the implications of their actions (DeMatthews, Mungal & Carrola, 2015). The choices to be made are perplexing, and may have competing sets of sources. Several factors may contribute to negative decision-making, including errors in judgement, insufficient information, failure to identify biases, and misinformation (Heffernan, 2015). Making a firm decision is difficult, and businesses are fluid institutions vulnerable to unforeseen problems. The society in which we operate is ever changing and fluid, leading to members not taking the time to pause for reflection. Taking additional time to consider data, people, and details that might have been overlooked, will allow possibilities and scenarios time to play out (Heffernan, 2015). Members may fail to identify the best decision because individuals on the committee cannot consider all possible alternatives, will back down to other member influences and pressures, or suffer from uncertainty and be unable to commit (DeMatthews et al., 2015). To ensure a decision is made, leadership helps members put events into context, draws out prior member experiences, and decides as a group the best plan of action (DeMatthews et al., 2015). It is challenging to establish partnerships and sustain a high level of enthusiasm. Common challenges that committees face are independent personalities, difficult stakeholders, and follow-through with commitments (DiMattina, n. d.). The ways and constructs with which advisory committees operate may differ; there is no exact rule, because the members and their experiences are unique and separate (Pettigrew, 2014). A well-intended group can make bad decisions that result in negative effects. As a group, members analyze possible courses of action, discuss the potential outcomes, and take into consideration the possible consequences of their decisions (DeMatthews et al., 2015). Utilizing a strong leader to discuss these actions will lead the group toward accomplishing its goal. Before leading the group to a final discussion, the leader should make sure he or she has the most accurate and complete information available, and check first for any others wishing to voice their ideas (DeMatthews et al., 2015).

Including a leader who conforms to the belief that there is always room for improvement will keep the program current and relevant. A member dedicated to the entire process—that is, following the project through from its start and until the program is no longer needed—is vested and committed to the success of the project. As part of the overall program, the advisory committee should incorporate review TET evaluation regarding the need and function of the project each year, as a necessary component. Adding a leader who knows what to ask and how to ask questions can keep the discussions on track, and ascertain relevant information (C. Walker, personal communication, April 6, 2015). A dedicated leader can probe for further information and assess what meets community needs—a vital component of the committee leader.

TEAM APPROACH

The advisory committee is organized as a team, working together as a group of decision-makers, not as independent leaders or power struggles. In order for the team to develop their skills and work effectively, the appointed team leader will create a professional rapport with the members. The members should be well-informed and communication be open and fluid. Working as a team, the group will operate as solution-oriented with a clear goal and expectations outlined to all members upon selection. The leadership should make sure no member is singled out or criticized, therein, encouraging open and honest participation by each member. Remember – each member has been selected for their expertise and are a necessary component on the committee; nonetheless, not all individuals are comfortable sharing information in a public setting. This is where the team approach works well using other members to encourage or help speak-up for those reluctant to share their ideas. Separating into smaller individual groups will also help with this approach.

Advisory committee members are selected based on their professional experience and are therefore likely to be making decisions within their own companies and businesses that they are involved with and operate under strict time restraints. Hence, it is important to respect their time by assigning each member individual tasks to accomplish by way of setting deadlines all must adhere to. A situation may arise in which members are called away on out-of-town trips or personal issues; therefore, pairing up members to work together outside of the collective meeting may be necessary. This collaboration between members would allow for the advisory committee to continue its task and meet the set deadline by relaying the information to the group. The leader may also need to visit with individual members at their place of business to obtain information from a member to share at the next meeting and offer follow-up information to the group for those unable to attend each meeting. The members of each advisory committee will have unique and different personalities as they deal with others on the committee. It is common to find that leadership and management styles vary.

Unfortunately, the need for conflict resolution may become an issue within the committee. Conflicts need to be dealt with swiftly because they can have a negative impact of the effectiveness of the overall committee (Hashish et al., 2015). The members have been chosen because they have knowledge and expertise that is of importance to the committee's goal; however, not all will be willing to work alongside other members. Some may be presidents and owners that are not accustomed to sharing information and resources as a group. A decisive leader will help negotiate these conflicts. Sometimes appointing another member to work with the individual or explaining privately the reasoning working as a team is important to the overall goal may be necessary (Northouse, 2013). If an individual continues to disrupt the rapport of the group dynamics, it may become necessary to remove the individual from the committee or ask they give input through written communication instead of attending the meetings. The connection the members feel to one another and the task at hand is important to the overall success of the project (Northouse, 2013). Resolving and addressing the conflict at the onset by using effective and constructive management will deter any disruption to the dynamics of the committee (Hashish et al., 2015).

As discussed earlier in the works of Follett (1918), some conflict within teams can be beneficial. Follett (1918) explained that conflict has the potential to improve decision-making. Moderate conflict within teams can prevent a group from becoming stagnant and unproductive (Follett, 1918). The focus of the issue can become clearer and spark new discussions. When teams work cohesively together they give members more latitude to express their opinions without being personally insulted (McShane and Von Glinow, 2014). When members are able to hold their emotions at bay during a discussion, a conflict becomes constructive and team members appreciate the open and honest discussions instead of avoiding being forthright with one another (McShane and Von Glinow, 2014).

Delving specifically into organizational conflict, there are 4 identified as Rahim's model: intrapersonal, interpersonal, intragroup, and intergroup wherein conflict may occur (Rahim, 2011). For the purpose of this discussion and advisory committees - interpersonal and intragroup conflict will apply.

Interpersonal conflict may occur between individuals when there is a personality clash or disagreement often brought on because of hierarchical stature (Rahim, 2011). Rahim (2011) suggest using open communication, clarifying the misunderstanding, and identifying the cause of the conflict.

The other conflict, intragroup occurs within groups erupting because of disagreements regarding a task, solution, goal, or ways to approach solutions (Rahim, 2011). Rahim (2011) recommends leaders acknowledge there is no right or wrong answers or no one group is the winner or loser over others. A dominating leader will address compromising with the group or individual and address issues openly. Working with a group of individuals regarding high-stake decision-making is challenging, but can lead to effective results.

CONSEQUENCES

There are certainly consequences to remaining inactive and not making a decision. It might appear to be the safest course of action; however, business and industry know all too well that if you wait, someone else will find a way to make changes, and then the project or program becomes obsolete. Making the right decision is difficult for even the highest level of executives. It requires individuals who seek out answers, set aside differences, and ultimately work together to produce a program or project in which they are vested as a group (Langley, 2015). It is important to include individuals on the committee who have a strong ability to motivate members, and just as important to eliminate sceptics and those who always see things negatively. Another advantage to including multiple business and industry managers, CEOs, presidents, and administrators, is that they are used to facing a multitude of challenges on a continual and fluid basis. These leaders also realize that poor decisions have a direct effect on business/industry bottom lines. Heffernan (2015) points out that 47% of unsuccessful projects are due to poor decisions. In her studies of effective decisions, Heffernan (2015) reveals there are five methodical approaches to effective decision-making, as discussed in A Guide to the

Project Management Body of Knowledge (PMBOK Guide), of which three are examined below for advisory members:

1. **Problem Definition:** Fully explore, clarify, and define the problem.
2. **Problem Solution Generation:** Brainstorm multiple solutions.
3. **Solutions Evaluation Planning:** Perform a postimplementation analysis and evaluation of the lessons learned.

Before making a decision, the entire membership should be well informed of the problem, possible outcomes, and consequences, and any limits placed upon the program or project. Using all the members, to share with the committee through brainstorming the solutions, possible issues, expenses, facilities, availability, and possibility of success, helps generate a healthy discussion to arrive at productive solutions. And finally, the committee should perform a post analysis of the decisions made. Included in the analysis should be a candid discussion of the lessons learned. This final step is often forgotten or dismissed as unnecessary; nonetheless, there will be other discussions in the future that will hinge on what was learned previously.

Keep in mind, not all approaches are a good fit for each committee, and there is no "one size fits all." Going in with a plan and making adjustments as needed throughout the duration of the committee's existence is part of an ongoing process. The goal is to make the best, cohesive working committee for a particular project or program. It is important to remember that decisions a committee makes today will have implications and consequences for 8 to 10 years into the future (Heffernan, 2015). Utilizing a methodical approach gives a committee, especially a newly formed one, a guideline to which to adhere, and from which to make adjustments as needed. And finally, when educational institutions are involved, it is imperative that the committee remembers to keep the institution's mission statement aligned with the strategy the committee wants to implement.

MEDICAL PATIENT DECISION-MAKING

Decision-making is not only a part of business and industry, but also infuses lives. Patients are getting more involved and taking an active role in decision-making regarding their medical treatments. The complexity of choices overwhelms many patients deciding on a treatment or surgical option. Healthcare providers are making a conscious effort to help inform and walk patients through all their choices; explaining risk, translating difficult wording, allowing full access to medical records, and presenting statistics related to the procedures (Landro, 2017). University of Utah research shows that communication and active participation in decision-making by patients results in 5.3% lower medical expenses, and 12.5% fewer elective surgeries (Landro, 2017). The patients getting more involved in the decision-making with their doctors are more likely to follow treatments, suggestions, and recommendations by their medical staff. Patients are finding new interactive programs and videos outlining benefits and risk involved in any treatment and procedures, in comprehensible terms. Multiple treatments are explained in layman's terms, using comparative charts with visual aids and thorough explanations. The new shared decision-making process between doctor and patient has also relieved concerns for doctors. If the patient chooses not to follow the doctor's recommendations, the patient has been fully informed of the risks and benefits, removing the concern from the doctor. The added information and communication available to patients through decision-making is decreasing the overwhelming and powerless feeling, giving patients a voice to make informed decisions regarding their medical needs, instead of the doctor making the decisions in isolation.

For years, individuals have been urged to get involved with decisions regarding their own medical care, but deciphering the medical information was beyond the ability of the typical patient to understand. Terminology used in medical records is difficult to grasp, and information is only partially available, as much of the data was redacted. Now providers are making available equipment and sites with better tools, to help patients with their decision-making. Shared decision-making between the doctor and patients is putting patients in control of their own medical decisions. By making complex medical terminology and information available in simpler words and more easily accessible, the medical community is including the patient in the treatment discussion.

CONCLUSION

It is difficult to replace or find a substitute for an individual who is a sound decision-maker, a leader who makes decisions built on experience tested through the years. Even with the aid of technology that reveals the most efficient solutions, a well-tested and practiced leader's judgement is more successful, and has more ability to justify, learn, and adjust to mistakes and find solutions than a computerized program does (Greenwald, 2017). Technology is taking over in many areas, resulting in great strides toward saving money and time. Nonetheless, within the realm of decision-making, there is no evidence that technology can make decisions that are as good as, or even better than skilled individuals. There is no guaranteed system, and it may be years, if ever, before a systematic process can be developed that is an automated decision-maker replacing the skills, experience, and judgment of managers and administrators (Greenwald, 2017). The technology-driven automation may be appealing to companies, but this is one area where one's own judgment and justification cannot be replaced.

Typically, not all individuals are skilled decision-makers, because they react instinctively instead of taking their time and critically reasoning through the process. Using a structured, systematic course of action to reason through and analyze the underlying problem, using best practices, results in productive decisions. This chapter discussed the many problems and factors facing decision-makers, and how to apply best practices to making an informed decision, not only in business and industry, but also in one's personal life.

Including talented, experienced, and knowledgeable members on the committee who already have proven decision-making skills will be an overall advantage to the success of the team. Decisions will be made as a team, with no one member coming out on top or making anyone any more successful or powerful than the program. Combining a group of intelligent individuals who can work harmoniously with one another, and ask questions of the group, community, and experts in the field, will lead to accurate decisions. This same conclusion was realized in the medical community, which is working to include the individual in the decision by giving patients a clearer understanding, providing precise data accompanied by explanations. The same decision-making skills carry over into business and industry, as well as to personal lives.

In the 1960s, engineer W. Edwards Deming made the statement, "In God we trust; all others must bring data." There is truth and methodology in this quote as a guide to decision-making. Data is a necessary component; however, it must be turned into knowledge before taking action (Deming, 1986). Do your homework— collect all the data possible, including interviewing, networking, discussions, facts, and even visiting facilities, before placing your reputation, money, and energies in committing to a project.

REFERENCES

Allingham, M. (2002). *Choice Theory*. New York, NY: Oxford University Press. doi:10.1093/actrade/9780192803030.001.0001

Bess, J. L., & Dee, J. R. (2008). *Understanding college and university organizations: Theories for effective policy and practice* (Vol. II). City, VA: Stylus.

Bray, J. (2011, January 17). Career and technical colleges can help retrain the unemployed. *The Chronicle of Higher Education*. Retrieved from http://chronicle.com/article/CareerTechnical-Colleges/125977/

Brown, R. A., & Shen, H. (2017). Challenges and solutions of higher education in the Eastern Caribbean States. Retrieved from https://eric.ed.gov/?q=higher+education+networking&ft=on&id=EJ1126023

Burke, L., & Miller, M. (1999). Taking the mystery out of intuitive decision-making. Retrieved from http://aspnet.cob.ohio.edu/mc/pmba_co_3/Class/CMBA602Strategic/TheMaterialReadings/Module%202%20Readings/R%234%20Taking%20the%20Mystery%20out%20of%20Intuitive%20Decision%20Making.pdf

Carlson, P., Holm, R., & Uvalde, R. (2011). Building regional partnerships for economic growth and opportunity. Jobs for the Future. Retrieved from http://futureworks-web.com/pdfs/Building_RegionalPartnerships.pdf

Day, M. (2001). Faculty perceptions of advisory committee effectiveness at two-year technical college. *Journal of Education for Business*, *110*(2), 194–198.

DeMatthews, D., Mungal, A., & Carrola, P. (2015, Winter). Despite best intentions: A critical analysis of social justice leadership and decision making. *Administrative Issues Journal.*, *5*(2), 17–37. doi:10.5929/ 2015.5.2.4

Deming, E. (1986). *Out of the Crisis*. Cambridge, MA: MIT Press.

Deming, W. E. (1994). *The New Economics for Industry, Government and Education*. Cambridge: MAMIT Press.

DiMattina, C. (n. d.). Lessons in collaboration: Principles in the governance of an industry advisory board. Retrieved from https://www.acteonline.org/uploadedFiles/Assets_and_Documents/Global/files/Publications/RPB_IndustryAdvisoryBoards.pdf

Dixon, H. (1990). *Communication.* Houston, TX: Washington and Lee University.

Dougherty, K. J., & Townsend, B. K. (2006). Community college missions: A theoretical and historical perspective. New Direction for Community Colleges, (136), 5-13.

Follett, M. P. (1918). *Group Organization.* New York, NY: Longmans, Green and Company.

Greenstone, M., & Looney, A. (2011). *Building America's job skills with effective workforce programs: A training strategy to raise wages and increase work opportunities.* The Hamilton Project. Retrieved from http://www.brookings.edu/~/media/research/files/papers/2011/11/training%%20 looney/11_training_greenstone_looney.pdf

Greenwald, T. (2017). How AI is transforming the workforce. *Workplace Technology. The Wall Street Journal. 13 March 2017.R1.*

Hamilton, V. (2004). *Building communities with a competitive workforce advantage. Sustaining Partnerships for Regional Economic Growth* (pp. 30–34). Washington, D.C.: American Association of Community Colleges.

Hashish, E. A., Hamouda, G. M., & Taha, E. (2015). Nursing students' perception of conflict management styles of their nursing educators. Retrieved from https://eric.ed.gov/?q=conflict+management+with+committees&id=EJ1079105

Heffernan, M. (2015). Making effective decisions. PMI's Pulse of the Profession. Retrieved from https://www.pmi.org/learning/thought-leadership/pulse/capturing-the-value-of-project-management

Hodges, R. (2012). *The road half traveled.* East Lansing, MI: Michigan State University Press.

Johnson, N., Oliff, P., & Williams, E. (2011). An update on state budget cuts. Retrieved from http://www.mobilelottery.com/wp-content/uploads/2010/05/Update-On-State-Budget-Cuts.pdf

Johnson, N., Oliff, P., & Williams, E. (2011). An update on state budget cuts. Retrieved from http://www.mobilelottery.com/wp-content/uploads/2010/05/Update-On-State-Budget-Cuts.pdf

Jones, G. (2006). *Organizational theory design and change* (5th ed.). Saddle River, NJ: Prentice Hall.

Kerka, S. (2002). *Effective advisory committees.* [ERIC Information Analyses ED463411]. Retrieved from ehis.ebscohost.com.lib-e2.lib.ttu.edu

Kilcrease, K. M. (2011). Faculty perceptions of business advisory boards: The challenge for effective communication. *Journal of Education for Business, 86*(2), 78–83. doi:10.1080/08832323.2010.480989

Kokkonen, L., & Almonkari, M. (2015). Teaching networking: An interpersonal communication competence perspective. Received from https://eric.ed.gov/?q=higher+education+networking&ft=on&id=ED565025

Landro, L. (2017). How to (really) get patients to take more control over their medical decisions. *Wall Street Journal.* 27 February 2017. R1.

Langley, M. (2015). Making effective decisions. PMI's Pulse of the Profession. Retrieved from https://www.pmi.org/learning/thought-leadership/pulse/capturing-the-value-of-project-management

Lewis, M. (2017). *The Undoing Project.* New York, NY: W.W. Norton & Company.

Lu, P. et al., (2016). National and State-Specific Td and Tdap Vaccination of Adult Populations.

McShane, S., & Von Glinow, M. (2014). *Organizational Behavior.* New York, NY: McGraw-Hill Companies, Inc.

Mele, D. (2006). Follett's organizational approach. Retrieved from http://www.iese.edu/research/pdfs/DI-0618-E

Metcalf, H., & Urwick, M. (2013). *Dynamic administration: The collected papers of Mary Parker Follett. Mansfield Centre.* CT: Martino Publishing.

Northouse, P. G. (2013). *Leadership: Theory and practice.* Los Angeles, CA: Sage Publishing.

Pettigrew, A. M. (2014). *The politics of organizational decision-making.* New York, NY: Routledge.

Price, D. V., & Roberts, B. (2009). Improving student success by strengthening developmental education in community colleges: The role of state policy. The Working Poor Families Project. Retrieved from http://www.workingpoorfamilies.org/pdfs/WPFP_policybrief_winter08-09.pdf

Rahim, M. A. (2011). Managing conflict in organizations. Retrieved from http://enactskills.eu/wordpress /en/learning-materials/interpersonal-conflict/

Smith, P. (2013). *Creative Experience: Mary Parker Follett*. Mansfield Center, CT: Martino Publishing.

Soares, L. (2010). The power of the education-industry partnership. Retrieved from http://americanprogress.org/issues/labor/report/2010/10/04/8518/thepoweroftheeducation

Spector, B. (2012). *Implementing organizational change: Theory into practice* (3rd ed.). Saddle River, NJ: Prentice Hall.

Tonn, J. (2003). *Mary P. Follett: Creating democracy, transforming management*. New Haven, CT: Yale Publishing. doi:10.12987/yale/9780300096217.001.0001

ADDITIONAL READING

Bontrager, B. (2008). *STEM and institutional success: Integrating enrollment, finance, and student access*. Retrieved from http://consulting.aacrao.org/publications-events/publications/sem-and-institutional-success-reviewed-in-aacraos-college-and-university-journal/

Brint, S., & Karabel, J. (1991). *The Diverted Dream*. New York, NY: Oxford University Press.

Combs, S. (2010). Texas ahead. Retrieved from http://www.texasahead.org/reports/incentives/sdf.php

Higher Education for Democracy. (1947). *The President's commission higher education for democracy 1947*. New York, NY: Harper & Brothers: Retrieved from http://courses.education.illinois.edu/eol474/ sp98/truman.html

Levin, J., & Kater, S. (2012). *Understanding Community Colleges*. New York, NY: Routledge.

KEY TERMS AND DEFINITIONS

Accountability: A policy of holding schools and teachers accountable for students' academic progress by linking such progress with funding for salaries, maintenance, and a means to measure the progress with a set of standards.

Advisory Committee: A selected group of leaders who provide knowledge and guidance to the development and continuity of community-college workforce educational programs, biomedical education, and business and industry.

Inclusion: The act of including someone or something as a part of something larger, a group, or a list.

Networking: The exchange of information or services among individuals, groups, or institutions.

Occupational: Relating to a person's job or profession.

Organizational Approach: Based on the organization's needs, a conceptual construct based on general systems theory.

Oversight Board: Body within the department of education that provides general governance, supervision, and support.

Practitioners: A person engaged in the practice of a profession or occupation.

Programmatic Design: Precise project footprints or specific design.

Reciprocal Relationships: Relationships that require participants to mutually participate and do something similar for each party that is mutually beneficial to both parties.

Seamless Transition: Establishing a high level of interagency collaboration that is an effective way to ensure that students transfer from high schools to post-secondary educational institutions.

Stakeholder: Anyone having an interest in a project, such as investors, employees, customers, suppliers, students, administrators, faculty, businesses, industry, and individuals.

Sustainable Economic Development: Measures the country's well-being and how well a country is performing to improve or sustain the dimensions of development, based on data.

Chapter 4
Advisory Committees in Biomedical Research and Training

Argentina Ornelas
University of Texas MD Anderson Cancer Center, USA

ABSTRACT

Biomedical Research Training falls under the umbrella of Graduate Education at higher education institutions. The extent that advisory committees play in such training is not well documented, as these change from institution to institution. The National Institutes of Health (NIH), the guiding federal agency that provides the bulk of financial support to biomedical research institutions, provides input in training and workforce development based on the research of their internal advisory committees. Discussed is the background of advisory committees in guiding graduate education and the roles of advisory committees in biomedical research education and training. Discussed are the roles of advisory committees at various levels of biomedical research education and training, from funding agencies (NIH), to advisory committees guiding training programs and delivering trainee advice at individual institutions. Discussion of the challenges in establishing advisory committees to develop a productive biomedical research workforce will ensue, as we shift from educational training to workforce development.

DOI: 10.4018/978-1-5225-4083-0.ch004

ADVISORY COMMITTEES IN BIOMEDICAL RESEARCH EDUCATION

The fundamental goal of biomedical research training is to incite and encourage the discovery of solutions to key biomedical problems through the scientific, evidence-based approach of research investigation; a trial-and-error approach that requires collective and multidisciplinary support from various groups, departments, and institutions. To guide this principle, the use of advisory committees is fundamental to establish collaborations, improve communication, and establish a fast-failure environment conducive to the overall assessment and immediate feasibility of research projects. In biomedical research education, advisory committees are essential to the fundamental training component, and to the advancement of projects in various areas of investigation (basic research, preclinical research, clinical research, case and cohort/epidemiological studies, collaboration between labs, technique and skill acquisition, manuscript preparation and publication, student dissertation and thesis projects). Advisory committees are also instrumental in the development of knowledge and impact of diverse areas of biomedical interest (epidemic or pandemic current diseases, public health concerns, improvements in population health), as well as implementation and evolution of larger-scale health initiatives (Cancer Moonshot initiatives – Federal and Institutional). Advisory committees in biomedical research serve to align the principles, knowledge, interests, goals, and ideas within a number of individuals who hold a special interest in the improvements and advancements in a particular field of the biomedical enterprise. The biomedical enterprise is a diverse system consisting of bench, preclinical and clinical research discoveries that will improve patient care and public health. The aim is to align the most pressing needs in health issues and disparities with the current and developing innovation happening at different institutions across the nation. Furthermore, the biomedical enterprise requires a number of highly trained individuals capable of understanding the major points in a number of arenas; from carrying out the biomedical science in question, to the translation and communication of such science and its findings to the population. To advance the biomedical research enterprise, it is therefore necessary that an education provide interdisciplinary guidance, to which we argue, can best be provided with a combination of ideas, knowledge and interests from a number of related venues. Advisory committees then, are an ideal vehicle to best serve in providing the guidance to advance educational goals in biomedical research.

At various academic institutions across the nation, a wide number of programs offer biomedical research training. Such academic research programs, have become the cornerstone of distinguished scholarship that is necessary to make advances in a wide range of areas that affect health outcomes (Research Universities Consortium). Academic research has become an enterprise that has incrementally developed to maximize functionality and productivity (Research Universities Consortium). Although the management of such institutions differs greatly, at the heart of guidance of research programs, there are a number of similarities that abound between all the institutions across the United States. The use of advisory committees is highly ubiquitous. As discussed in earlier chapters, advisory committees abound in guiding technical programs in community colleges, and it is in biomedical research education, that at the highest (federal), and lowest (thesis committee) levels of management, their utilization is critical in guiding desired outcomes.

At the core of advisory committees is the selection and appointment of a diverse group of individuals to function on behalf of a larger group. Sensibly, a larger body entrusts a smaller subset of well-versed members to represent, advocate and find resolutions to issues that the otherwise larger group could not effectively and expediently address. Establishing advisory committees will often be defined in organizational by-laws or statutes and formation of these committees come with specific and defined functions for advocacy and discussion. Some committees are enduring, and the continuity in advisory committees allows this group to address a multitude of issues that arise over the course of time, with no fixed endpoint. Typically, advisory committees are headed by a committee chair and will be composed of individuals representing different points of view (junior and full faculty), different organizational components (departments and/or divisions), or different constituencies (female basic research scientists and/or postdoctoral scholars) (Grigsby, 2008). Advisory committees are fundamental in higher education; however, their impact in biomedical research training does not often reflect the diversity in view point, organizational components, or in its constituents. In many cases, the reach of an advisory committee can be limiting, and the effect of such limitations can result in lack of diversity in representation. It is therefore necessary that in biomedical research education advisory committees, the various individuals and entities affected by the reach of an advisory committee be represented. An advisory committee in biomedical research education, needs to be well represented by different points of view (faculty on all levels of career), organizational components (student graduate programs and departmental faculty), and diverse constituency (foreign research/graduate students and domestic). It is also necessary to identify the major stakeholders that have active participation in delivering input and guidance, and are active in the promotion of employment after a graduate training career (academia, industry, government research, non-profits) and encourage their participation in such committees.

It is therefore important to note that advisory committees guide biomedical research education. At the simplest levels, advisory committees are utilized to guide a thesis research project. This relies on a group of well-established research faculty; whose main operative is to guide and assess a trainee's research project. This type of advisory committee has been used for many years in biomedical research training, and it is imperative to question whether this same format in guiding a biomedical research education has become archaic. In the early stages of their training, young investigators or trainees rely on the unquestioned input from research faculty to guide projects, coursework, resources and advocacy. Biomedical research education has been formatted to follow such format so that a research faculty becomes the supporter and primary mentor during a phase of training. However, it has become more apparent that there must be additional input from outside sources in order to improve the exploratory component that biomedical research education should provide (Alberts, 2014; Alberts, 2015; Daniels, 2015; Rodgers, 2013).

A publication from Alberts in 2014 (Alberts, 2014), and a follow-up discussion in 2015 (Alberts, 2015) denotes the major issues in biomedical research and its dwindling decline as a career prospect. In the past 10-20 years, there has been increased issues with the methods and systems that seem to indicate that biomedical research education is not the scholastic pinnacle it once was (Daniels, 2015). The problem is the limiting issues that restrict the workforce opportunities that previously abounded the field upon completing a rigorous training phase and conferment of a degree. One major huddle in the impact of the training component of biomedical research is the lack of input and associations from the major stakeholders in developing complete and diverse advisory committees in biomedical research.

The utilization of advisory committees has been more notably utilized in guiding community college education. Advisory committees are instrumental in establishing training programs, as well as in recruiting and involving community resources. The feedback of advisory committees allows the development and implementation of courses and curricula designed to meet the current demands in a specialized and technical niche. In higher education and in particular in the training of biomedical researchers in graduate programs, academic institutions are the principal stakeholders in designing a program to meet the needs of the institution, while the immediate surrounding community plays very little or no role in guiding training programs. In biomedical research education, there are two critical stakeholders that provide little or no input in training opportunities and development.

There are a variety of factors that deters the collaboration between major stakeholders in the development of a sustainable biomedical research enterprise, including: the cultural differences at every level of academia, industry and government, their funding practices, the unclear differentiation of goals, the coordination and integration of a trained workforce, to name a few. At best, academia is the principal stakeholder in the process of developing a multifaceted, multidisciplinary and diverse biomedical research workforce that meets the demands of investigators at specific institutions. But knowing full well the increased supplied of researches and the limited opportunities to fill in the academic workforce are in discord, it is essential, vital and responsible to the formation of advisory committees that can encompass a training research education to meet the demands of all groups that benefit from the development of a biomedical research workforce: Academia, Industry and Government.

A number of professional associations, like the American Society for Biochemistry and Molecular Biology (ASBMB), the Federation of American Societies of Experimental Biology (FASEB), the American Chemical Society (ACS) and the federal grants issuing agency, the National Institutes of Health (NIH) have recognized the disconnect between the development of a sustainable biomedical research enterprise, and the reality faced by the biomedical research workforce. The biomedical research enterprise that relies heavily in the trained community, requires improvements in its advisory committees to better serve the training body. The initiation of a dialogue between scientific societies, which often advocates for the professional needs of its members, and groups that require guidance (often its own membership base) can add a new dimension to the development of advisory committees.

One of the most appropriate solutions to improve the biomedical research training and workforce environment is to develop advisory committees that considers conflicts, provides knowledge and guidance, identifies issues and serves to disseminate assistance and recommendations to improve outcomes. At various levels, advisory committees in biomedical research are implemented, but there has never been a best-practices review on what has improved the different arenas of biomedical research. These arenas include discussions of the relevant training that should be provided by biomedical research institutions, forecasting the development of a workforce in biomedical research, and ensuring participation from a variety of stakeholders to improve workforce outcomes.

THE TRICKLING EFFECT OF ADVISORY COMMITTEES: FROM GUIDING COUNCILS TO GRADUATE PROGRAMS

The impact and magnitude of the role of advisory committees in biomedical research education is not well established, and their application to the improvement of programs and projects can only be described as severely underestimated and underutilized. As mentioned previously, a number of professional organizations advocate for their own member-base. Often times the representation of specific groups in advisory committees improves the outreach that would otherwise not be present. FASEB often provides a number of recommendations to biomedical research advisory committees to improve the quality of training and the experience (FASEB, 2015). It cannot be stated enough that advisory committees are increasingly ubiquitous in developing training programs. In addition, their use by professional societies that are associated with biomedical research, advisory committees benefit by the continual involvement from the general public (Pramesh, 2016). Biomedical research is seen as exceedingly crucial for the progress and the health of its population. It is also important to note that based on the perspectives of the general population, the funding resources will change dramatically.

An additional source in helping to shape the public perceptions of biomedical research are advisory committees that work at the federal level. Over a 1000 committees advise the federal government in a diverse number of fields including those dealing with scientific, technical and medical issues (Steinbrook, 2004). It is generally expected that any scientific advice that originates in advisory committees at this level, be protected from the influence of politics. Federal scientific advisory committees are meant to provide independent, expert and objective advice to improve policy and funding. The implications that this advisory committees have on biomedical research education is often seen in grant availability that helps support the research enterprise.

Finally, funding institutions like the NIH also make use of advisory committees to guide biomedical research education and workforce. Publications from such committees, such as the Draft Report of the Advisory Committee to the Director working Group on Diversity in the Biomedical Research Workforce (WGDBRW, 2012), serve to provide data, support, research findings to improve programs and strengthen the biomedical research workforce.

ADVISORY COMMITTEES IN GUIDING EDUCATIONAL ENTITIES

The Council for Graduate School (CGS), serves as the national voice for the Graduate Dean community at the various higher education institutions granting Masters and Philosophy Doctorate degrees in the United States. Research universities that heavily invest in the education and training of biomedical research are part of this council. The council serves as the national organization for graduate programs in the United States and Canada, and it is dedicated to the advancement of graduate education and research. It is through this national organization that advocacy for a variety of issues are brought to the spotlight. Many of the issues brought up by the Council for Graduate School encompass the policy arena, the development of innovative research, and advocating for the growth and dissemination of best practices. These are also issues that advisory committees within the Council for Graduate Schools address on a regular basis, and in fact, there is implementation of advisory committees that spearhead these issues. Many of the issues that warrant the implementation to advisory committees include and are not limited to advancement, directorate and office issues, masters research and framework, best practices and benchmarking.

Interestingly the Council for Graduate Schools makes use of advisory committees to provide the associated member institutions and the deans for graduate education and associated stakeholders with the tools to establish best practices for programs. Through the use of advisory committees, the Council for Graduate Schools is able to provide information to member institutions for benchmarking, best practices, advocacy, public policy, and the resources for global engagement. In addition, there is also a bridge that is formed between the council of graduate schools and corporations and non-profit organizations that actively participate and invest in graduate education.

There are four major core activity initiatives that the council of graduate schools spearhead to member institutions. At the forefront are best practices initiatives, which seek to draw on the leadership and research from graduate deans, so as to identify and implement best practices to the graduate education community. Under the umbrella of best practices, is the multi-university initiative to understand the PhD career pathways in the humanities and social sciences graduate programs. The current information on these statistics is typically drawn from national datasets such as the Survey on Earned Doctorates (SED) and the Survey on Doctorate Recipients (SDR). Yet as valuable as these surveys prove in demonstrating certain aspects of PhD careers at the national level, they lack the individual and specific program information to implement program improvements. The council for graduate schools also enhances the literature in best practices for graduate education by publication of career directives typically accessible to the member institutions.

The Council for Graduate Schools is also the leading authority in presenting and outsourcing information, data analysis and trends in graduate education. Through the benchmark core practice, the data provided by CGS helps member institutions assess the performance in key areas of education and training, make best decisions, and guides the development of plans suited to the end goals of each institution.

A third core activity guided by the CGS is the public policy and advocacy actions on issues concerning graduate education. The CGS serves as the leader to advocate for graduate education issues. It is also the leading resource for policy makers and other interested parties for graduate education, research and scholarship. Members of the council of graduate schools are at the forefront in the information that relates to the legislative process and in particular that which relates to graduate education. As for example, at the time this manuscript is being prepared, the CGS has issued analysis, statements and opinions on issues that impact graduate education, such as Tax Reform (CGS Tax Reform, 2017) and Executive Orders on Immigration (CGS Executive Order, 2017).

The fourth and final core activity by the CGS, is the implementation of setting up a global engagement community that involves international graduate educational leaders to identify global trends, and engage an international community in graduate education, research, scholarship and the development of the global workforce that is engaged in graduate education community.

With these core activities as the guiding principles for the purpose of the Council for Graduate Schools, the CGS has chartered advisory committees to provide guidance on issues of special importance to the organization, and to its member institutions. Topics of special importance are geared towards the development and benchmarking of best practices, advocacy for policies that keep at the forefront the improvement and innovation of scholarship, research and training of graduate education; as well as improve a sustainable global engagement that underscores the importance of international collaborations. The chartered advisory committees per the CGS include the Advancement Advisory Committee, the Advisory Committee on Advocacy and Public Policy, the Diversity and Inclusiveness Advisory Committee and the Master Committee and Master's Committee Research Advisory Group.

Perhaps one of the most crucial advisory committee within the CGS that proves a more direct connection to a stronger workforce development is the Advancement Advisory Committee. The Advancement Advisory Committee is fundamental in fueling the relationships that will directly result in developing the workforce from the resulting graduate education pool of the institutions which it serves. "Advancement" then, refers to the activities related to the development of novel and strategic relationships with the members of the CGS Sustaining Membership Network, as well as the Corresponding Affiliate Members of CGS. It is therefore necessary that all activities under the Advancement Advisory Committee be anchored by the educational needs of the CGS institutional members. There are three specific goals that are at the forefront of the CGS Advancement committee, two of which seek to develop partnerships with other sectors for increased collaboration and newfound relationships that academic institutions will benefit from in developing a new graduate workforce. At the same time, we cannot remiss the value additional sectors (non-profit, for profit and governmental) acquire through collaborations with academic and research institutions (European Commission, 2007). One goal is to establish opportunities for collaboration between CGS graduate deans and private and non-profit organizations. From a workforce perspective, this action can initially assist in the development of additional curriculum that is directed by the needs of outside entities and stakeholders, and in a larger scope, develop collaborations for innovation and partnership advancement between academia and other sectors. At the same time, a parallel goal is to improve the quality of CGS meetings and member services through and enhanced and expanded relationship with private and non-profit organizations. Through these parallel goals, the Advancement Advisory Committee specific responsibilities fall into the formation of relationships between academic, industry and government sectors. First, by advising on the development of CGS Advancement priorities, including providing insight into emerging areas of potential collaboration between graduate schools and industry; by advising on the development of strategies for meeting Advancement goals, including but not limited to advising on potential roles for partners and assessing the Sustaining Membership Networks; by facilitating relationships between CGS and external entities like non-profit organizations and for-profit companies; and by promoting CGS Advancement efforts within the graduate community.

CREATING PURPOSE, GOALS, EXPECTATIONS, AND METRICS FOR SUCCESS IN ADVISORY COMMITTEES IN BIOMEDICAL RESEARCH EDUCATION AND TRAINING

Advisory committees, task force groups, and teams are all created with perspectives and specific goals. Knowing the specific items and issues to endorse and advocate for within the specific committee or group, regardless of its descriptive title: biomedical workforce advisory committee or biomedical workforce task-force group, is far more important and valuable. This signifies that regardless of the name, the content and the items that need to be discussed and acted upon at this specific group are valuable and must come to a resolution in such matters within set timelines. Within a committee or a task-group, the selected individuals are tasked with very specific functions within the larger organization (Grigsby, 2006). In that sense, a larger body entrusts a select group of members to do something, analyze information, research an area of interest, and provide action and resolution to a specific cause. Advisory committees benefit from the support of the larger institution in gathering. In addition, the specific causes and items for the implementation of advisory committees are advanced with larger support. In the community college setting, advisory committees bridge the community workforce and the training facility and institutions to address the most important needs. These develop the needed rapport and open the communication with those seeking job opportunities and training, and business and professionals seeking to expand programs, fill vacant job opportunities, and increase the industrial enterprise. The industrial enterprise will change based on locality, interests of individuals and the health of an industry dependent on the current industry climate.

Biomedical education and research training is heavily carried out at a variety of higher learning institutions. The majority of this training and educational opportunities can start as early as secondary education (high school) and can continue through a briefer period, such as community college, or through a more specialized and prolonged time setting, such as pursuing a doctorate degree in biomedical sciences, which would typically last a period of 5-years and would follow an undergraduate education. There is extended encouragement to pursue biomedical research, and a number of groups, such as the National Institutes of Health (NIH) aim to improve workforce development by improving diversity in the biomedical and behavioral research. The means of improving diversity are by improving the statistics on minority underrepresentation in the biomedical and behavioral sciences and research. To achieve this, the NIH has developed the Working Group on Diversity in the Biomedical Research Workforce. This working group, acted on the auspices of the Advisory Committee to the Director of the NIH. The implementation of this working group, which can be additionally referred to as an advisory committee, has at its core interests, delivering an improved workforce in Biomedical Research, by improving and acting upon the increase in the enrollment of minority groups in the biomedical research field.

As expected from advisory committees, a number of recommendations were derived from the working group on diversity in the biomedical research workforce that will enhance the participation, diversity and improve the workforce statistics in this represented group. Some of the recommendations derived to in this report include.

1. Require that programs undergo a systematic review and evaluation every 5 years. Those found to be particularly effective in increasing Underrepresented Minorities participation in the biomedical sciences should be used as models for other programs that are not as effective, and should be considered for expansion.
2. Additional support should take the form of an increased number of scholarships for undergraduates that include 'payback' through participating in a meaningful research experience, and additional fellowships for the anticipated increased numbers of underrepresented minorities graduate students in biomedical research.
3. The NIH should partner with established scientific and professional groups and other trusted organizations to implement a system of mentorship 'networks' for underrepresented minority students that will provide career guidance through their career development.
4. Establishment of a working group on the Advisory Committee to the Director, of racially and ethnically diverse scientists, to provide regular input to the Director of the NIH, and the institutes and centers, regarding the state-of-the-art in effective programs that overcome or reduce disparities in research awards.

It is necessary to state that the educational and training component that these are only a few of the prescribed recommendations by the Working Group/Advisory Committed entrusted with developing recommendations and citing actionable items to enhance workforce development to a select community. This same implementation of advisory committee can be instituted in biomedical research education in order to improve the training and workforce development opportunities.

FOSTERING DIVERSITY IN ADVISORY COMMITTEES

Diversity in biomedical research is of upmost importance. Diversity is a centerpiece for establishing collaborative venues to advance the scientific enterprise. Diversity in the sciences implies a wide spectrum of opportunities to apply knowledge, contributions, ideas and disciplines effectively so as to expedite and advance scientific discoveries. In addition, this also allows the assessment of such discoveries when attempting to reach other areas. Diversity propagates when there are a number of contrasting agents or entities that provide novel problems and bring interdisciplinary collaboration. Advisory committees are the simplest most efficient method to improve the diversity spectrum.

In the Draft Report of the Advisory Committee to the Director Working Group on Diversity (WGDBRW, 2012), the case for increasing diversity focuses on bolstering creativity and achievement. Diversity is a key component of achievement, and is particularly conducive to innovation, when this one is a critical goal. The current work in the life sciences and in biomedical research education demands that innovation and creativity be at the forefront. The presence of diversity in advisory committees broadens the scope of inquiry to help expand questions that may be neglected by others. This fundamental principal can be associated with bringing a diverse set of knowledge and experiences. In addition, fostering a diverse advisory committee allows for improved interactions with outside participants. A diverse advisory committee lends itself to increased number of outside sources.

CHALLENGES OF ADVISORY COMMITTEES IN BIOMEDICAL RESEARCH EDUCATION AND TRAINING

There are a number of challenges that are associated with structuring, developing and sustaining advisory committees in biomedical research. Of these, the most prevalent is not entrusting an advisory committee to maintain diversity and limiting the participation of stakeholder entities into the decision-making process. Although there are effects of some advisory committees only serving until a specific issue is resolved, and at which point there are recommendation made to the guiding board or staff, there is a benefit in establishing a permanent advisory board or committee to provide the ongoing support. This has been crucial in community college in order to navigate the required workforce needs in a community. In biomedical research and training, although there are no community guiding principles, it is of great interest to establish a permanent advisory board to provide ongoing evaluations, assessments and guidelines to better serve the training community and establish a secure workforce. In providing trainees with increased connections with additional stakeholder groups, this leverages new opportunities for cooperation and improvement in outcomes.

DEVELOPMENT OF ADVISORY COMMITTEES IN BIOMEDICAL RESEARCH

At the Graduate School of Biomedical Sciences (GSBS) at University of Texas MD Anderson Cancer Center, advisory committees are guiding entities to improve the training, scholarship, education, experience and workforce development in up-and-coming biomedical scientists. The training component is guided in different disciplines all with a wide range of advising expertise in developing new generations of scientists, physician-scientists, and leading experts in cancer biology, novel therapies, treatments, and management. The University of Texas MD Anderson Cancer Center is a research hospital in Houston, Texas focused on advancing the treatment and health management on all fronts to battle cancer. The Graduate School of Biomedical Sciences (GSBS) is an associated institution with UT MD Anderson Cancer Center.

GSBS offers training with varying degrees of finality, these include a Master of Science Degree (M.S., a Doctor of Philosophy (Ph.D.), and a joint Medical Doctorate and Doctor of Philosophy (M.D.- Ph.D.).

Advisory committees at the community college level guides a larger organization, this one is often involved with the increased involved aspects of maintaining accountability on organizations funding apprenticeship programs, investing financial resources, enlisting local business expertise to guide existing programs or create new innovation. At the simplest level in the implementation of advisory committees in the Graduate School of Biological Sciences, these entities guide the educational and training component of fellows and trainees in the program. An advisory committee, specifically at the School of Biological Sciences, seeks to impart diversity, expertise, hypothesis development, mentoring, and scientific integrity, all as part of the individual training or just one trainee. With the opportunity to apply clinical, theoretical, translational and empirical training, the formulation of advisory committees at the School of Biomedical Sciences, enlists requirements that trainees must adhere to in preparation to developing their advisory council/committee.

The guiding principles and cores structure of advisory committees at individual institutions providing biomedical research training differ minimally within institutions in different programs, but also change remarkably little between institutions across the nation. This is to say, that the structure of an advisory committee at a biomedical research institution in the west coast, may be very similar as that fund in another institution in the east coast. What this presents is an issue that insinuates that advisory committees have changed remarkably little in how they have been used to provide biomedical research training.

Trainees, are typically encouraged to be active participants in the formation of their advisory committees. Below are the guidelines often associated with the structuring of a thesis advisory committee at the University of Texas Graduate School of Biomedical Sciences.

- A student/trainee is directly responsible for choosing an advisor to develop a research project.
- The research project will be the basis for training and this work will conclude with a written dissertation and a defense of such dissertation.
- The Advisory Committee bears primary responsibility for monitoring the Ph.D. trainee's progress and assists trainee in a number of milestones towards the completion of a degree. These milestones include:

  - Selection of relevant courses and coursework.
  - Development of a research program that includes a thesis and a hypothesis driven research plan.
  - Preparation for a candidacy exam and evaluation of work progress that will reflect proper preparation of trainee for an independent career and other workforce opportunities.
- After a candidacy phase, advisory committee becomes instrumental in monitoring progress until degree requirements are met.

Guidelines to Establishing Advisory Committees at The University of Texas MD Anderson Cancer Center Graduate School of Biomedical Sciences and at Baylor College of Medicine

The following are the guidelines towards the development of advisory committees with the underlying task of providing scientific consensus to the training of individuals undergoing biomedical research education and training.

- Advisory Committee consists of five members from the faculty staff.
- Advisory Committee is approved by primary mentor and reflects faculty members competent with the area of investigation.
- At least one member's research interests must lie outside the trainee's major discipline.
- At least one member must be outside the trainee's department.
- At least one member must be outside the trainee's program.
- At least one member must have extensive experience with GSBS student committees.
- Any one individual may meet one or more of these criteria.
- A non-faculty committee member is considered as a sixth, non-voting, member.

A number of institutions follow this patterns towards the educational and training component in biomedical and non-biomedical research and training. The end goals of implementing an advisory committee in education and training, much as it is observed in community colleges, is to develop a diverse setting that initiates and implements a number of solutions to specific issues and problems. In addition, an advisory committee leads in scope and prevents issues that may jeopardize the smooth trans-course between education and training components and the transition to workforce. In biomedical research education, it is important to foster a collaborative environment where projects progress, this is the basis of advancement in health outcomes and improvements. Also, important, is to incur a scientific curiosity with a diverse set of skills in trainees in order to be able to enter a biomedical research workforce. Many of the advances in biomedical research are initiated in an academic setting, but it is in an industrial atmosphere that projects advance and develop.

One of the issues that has been present in advisory committees in biomedical research education and training, is the involvement of stakeholder groups to guide training aspects and components. In addition, there is further need to involve the stakeholder parties to improve the workforce development and issues regarding workforce training, technology transfer, education, regulatory burden and product development.

OTHER ADVISORY COMMITTEES IN BIOMEDICAL RESEARCH EDUCATION AND TRAINING, AND WORKFORCE DEVELOPMENT

Challenges in emerging systems in biomedical research training have drawn considerable attention. In particular, is the persistent decline in purchasing power of the NIH funding, which undoubtedly affects the entire scientific workforce. For early career biomedical investigators, the period between conferral of a doctoral degree and the receipt of an independent research grant has widened by almost a decade. This presents a tightening of opportunities for careers in academia, and a lack of well-developed pipelines for alternative careers in industry and other non-academic settings. While there has been dedicated literature and considerable time to addressing these issues in a number of mediums, most recommendations to date have been focused on the role of NIH and less on the role that research universities – the institutions where vast majority of biomedical scientists train or work – must pay close devotion to finding a solution.

Advisory committees that focus on developing career opportunities for newly trained biomedical research scientists will provide opportunities for a population that may not be aware of the workforce opportunities available after completion of a terminal degree. Many institutions providing biomedical research education are slowly becoming more aware of the importance of workforce development as part of biomedical research training. In addition, a number of additional set of skill development must be provided. In the past decade, the focus has been in providing trainees with the scientific knowledge and technical skills to carry out needed experiments. This has now shifted by providing opportunities to understand and practice techniques in communication, entrepreneurship, project management; as well as the increased efforts to understand the various sectors for entering the workforce, academia, industry, government.

In addition, there are more interactions with trainee-focused groups to operate with more freedom in developing their own advisory committees for specific interest groups. For example, advisory committees have been developed to help guide and achieve specific interests for the trainee community, such as acquiring health benefits, parental leave, and protected time-off for job interviews. Such advisory committees are becoming increasingly present in biomedical research institutions, and trainees are understanding the need to assemble such groups with a diverse set of individuals.

The committee is especially entrusted to consider and draw on innovative practices and initiatives already underway in schools and divisions. Most importantly, it is focused on developing new models for graduate biomedical education that involves partnerships with outside stakeholders in order to cultivate diverse and pragmatic career skills. Some of the crafter rules and recommendations includes the duration of the graduate education and postdoctoral fellowships, advancement in new career development and mentoring initiatives for doctoral students, postdoctoral fellows and junior faculty.

Advisory Committees are instituted so as to solve characteristically, issues that can improve a number of problematic areas. In biomedical research, one of the most current and pressing issues has been the lack of career opportunities to doctoral trainees upon conferral of their degree. In a vigorous and challenging career, it should not be expected that additional challenges are non-existent, however, when there are still necessary opportunities to continue to train biomedical research trainees, there has to be opportunities to secure a job opportunity and obtain training that goes beyond the bench.

CONCLUSION

Educational advisory committees are instrumental in guiding an updated and practical curriculum to meet the academic needs at many institutions. In biomedical research education, an advisory committee carries out the same principles that are expected in other fields. Advisory committees in biomedical research education serves multiple goals depending on their specific purpose. Educational thesis advisory committees must provide longstanding guidance in research projects that will constitute for trainees, the completion and relevance of a research project. Such committees have changed very little in the past decades, an perhaps rethinking the way such advisory committees are formed will improve the functions that these are able to achieve. An advisory thesis committee is responsible for guiding trainees in the relevant training necessary to complete a graduate education. Aside from guidance in the training component, there is very little effect in an advisory committee will have in workforce development.

In the past decade, advisory committees have formed to help guide the graduate education at research institutions. The Council for Graduate Schools, as well as the Advisory Committee to the Director and the Working Group on Diversity in Biomedical Research Workforce, two committees streaming from the NIH, have reached out their functions to improve the workforce development in biomedical research.

These committees focus on developing ways to improve the biomedical research enterprise by improving the conditions of workforce development.

Other special interest advisory committees focus on extracurricular issues not directly related to biomedical research education. Instead, these are issues of special interest in advocacy and improvements for biomedical research trainees. Many of the benefits in having trainees as the work horse in the biomedical research workforce, is that these individuals receive quite a modest stipend in return for their training, yet many times the benefits are low, including compensation and health benefits.

In the next chapter, we analyze the impact of advisory committees in the biomedical research workforce and in its development. A discussion of advisory committees for education will be contrasted with the advisory committees that are focused on workforce training and development. In biomedical research, one of the most current and pressing issues has been the lack of career opportunities to doctoral trainees upon conferral of their degree. In a vigorous and challenging career, it should not be expected that additional challenges are non-existent, however, when there are still necessary opportunities to continue to train biomedical research trainees, there has to be opportunities to secure a job opportunity and obtain training that goes beyond the bench.

REFERENCES

Alberts, B., Kirschner, M. W., Tilghman, S., & Varmus, H. (2014). Rescuing US biomedical research from its systemic flaws. *Proceedings of the National Academies of Science.*, *111*(14), 5773–5777. doi:10.1073/pnas.1404402111 PMID:24733905

Alberts, B., Kirschner, M. W., Tilghman, S., & Varmus, H. (2015). Addressing systemic problems in the biomedical research enterprise. *Proceedings of the National Academies of Science.*, *112*(7), 1912–1913. doi:10.1073/pnas.1500969112 PMID:25691698

Council of Graduate Schools. (2017). Issue Brief: Tax Reform – Education Related Provisions. Retrieved from http://cgsnet.org/sites/default/files/Tax_reform_ISSUE_BRIEF_May_2017.pdf

Council of Graduate Schools. (2017). Updated: CGS Statement Regarding Administration's Executive Order on Immigration. Retrieved from http://cgsnet.org/updated-cgs-statement-regarding-administration%E2%80%99s-executive-order-immigration

Daniels, R. J. (2015). A generation at risk: Young investigators and the future of biomedical workforce. *Proceedings of the National Academies of Science.*, *112*(2), 313–318. doi:10.1073/pnas.1418761112 PMID:25561560

European Commission. (2007). Communications from the Commission: Improving knowledge transfer between research institutions and industry across Europe. Retrieved from http://ec.europa.eu/invest-in-research/pdf/download_en/knowledge_transfe_07.pdf

Federation of American Societies for Experimental Biology. (2015). *Sustaining discovery in biomedical and medical sciences: A framework for discussion.* Bethesda, MD, USA: FASEB.

Grigsby R.K. (2006). Are you really a team player? *Academic Physician and Scientist.* 4-5.

Grigsby, R. K. (2008). *Committee, Task Force, Team: What's the difference? Why Does It Matter?* (pp. 4–5). Academic Physician and Scientist.

Pramesh, C. S., Venkataramanan, R., Suvarna, V., Goel, N. S., Lakshman, S., Venkatesh, V., & Badwe, R. et al. (2016). Involvement of general public in biomedical research. *Perspectives in Clinical Research.*, *7*(4), 152–155. doi:10.4103/2229-3485.192029 PMID:27843788

Rodgers, B. D. (2013). When is education a disservice? *The FASEB Journal*, *27*(12), 4678–4681. doi:10.1096/fj.13-235762 PMID:23975933

Steinbrook, R. (2004). Science, Politics and Federal Advisory Committees. *The New England Journal of Medicine*, *350*(14), 1454–1460. doi:10.1056/NEJMhpr033416 PMID:15070798

The Research Universities Futures Consortium. (2012). *The Current Health and Future Well-Being of the American Research University*. Philadelphia, PA: Elsevier.

Working Group on the Diversity in the Biomedical Research Workforce (WGDBRW) and The Advisory Committee to the Director. (2012). Draft Report of the Advisory Committee to the Director Working Group on Diversity in the Biomedical Research Workforce. Retrieved from https://acd.od.nih.gov/documents/reports/DiversityBiomedicalResearchWorkforce Report.pdf

KEY TERMS AND DEFINITIONS

Biomedical Research Funding Agencies: Institutions, organizations or foundations responsible for funding and generating support for basic, translational, pre-clinical and clinical we identify the biomedical research stakeholders to be academia, industry and government.

Biomedical Research Stakeholders: Persons, entities and establishments that demonstrate deep interest and concerns into the development of biomedical field advancements. In this regard.

Biomedical Research Trainee: An individual seeking additional guidance and training in the field of biomedical research at a higher education institution, medical center, national laboratory. Such training concludes with the attainment of a higher degree, this being a Masters or a Doctorate. A trainee can be best identified as a graduate student or a postdoctoral fellow.

Biomedical Research Workforce: An entity that establishes the advancements, procedures, tasks and efforts in the biomedical field to advance new discoveries through investigation and trial-and-error procedures.

Council for Graduate Schools (CGS): Organization formed to account for the research and development of activities to advance graduate education and to promote U.S competitiveness in the global economy.

Graduate Student: An individual seeking a higher degree. In this publication, it refers to individuals in a biomedical research program with the expectation of completing such training to obtain a Masters or Doctorate degree.

Postdoctoral Fellow: An individual receiving further training after receiving a doctorate degree in the biomedical research field.

Workforce Diversity: Definition per NIH guidelines to improve diversity in the biomedical research field as addressed in the 2012 draft report on advisory committees to the director working group on diversity in the biomedical research workforce. Workforce diversity then is defined as the improvements in the recruitment and retention of underrepresented minorities, people with disabilities, and people from disadvantaged backgrounds across the lifespan of a biomedical research career.

Chapter 5
Development of a Biomedical Research Workforce Through the Support of Advisory Committees

Argentina Ornelas
University of Texas MD Anderson Cancer Center, USA

ABSTRACT

Workforce development has not always been a set goal in biomedical research education and training. The highly-specialized training in biomedical research has often focused on the development of academic focused scientists, however, in the past 20 years this has been observed as unsustainable. A discussion ensues of the key areas of improvement to develop a sustainable biomedical workforce, and improve dispersion of diverse talent in all areas of biomedical research training (academic, industrial and government). The roles of advisory committees in biomedical research education and training demands that these be extended to additional venues to improve workforce challenges as individuals leave the training phase. Involvement of stakeholder roles in training opportunities by opening collaborations with training institutions opens venues for improvements in educational relationships, and workforce improvements. This chapter will also address the value of biomedical research (VOBR) and discuss recommendations to address workforce diversity and development.

DOI: 10.4018/978-1-5225-4083-0.ch005

DEVELOPMENT OF A BIOMEDICAL RESEARCH WORKFORCE

To achieve diversity in the biomedical research workforce, it is critical to ensure that the best and the brightest minds have the opportunity to contribute to the realization of the national biomedical and clinical research goals. These goals promote an increase stability public health outcomes in the general population, as well as maintain positive financial outcomes. The American biomedical research enterprise is the world leader in health-related discovery and innovation, however the downturn in investment funds, in addition with a lagging biomedical research workforce that is not well compensated for its services, can change the prospects of continuing advancements in innovation, positives outcomes in public health, and workforce stability. The National Institutes of Health (NIH), the leading agency to support the efforts of biomedical research and dissemination of information to improve health outcomes, ensures that the development of a training campaign at all the institutions that receive federal funding, realizes a sustainable workforce. Typically, in biomedical research training, the apex of professional success after an intense training program, is a position of professorship in academia. This so called ivory tower has been eluded more recently by increased numbers of highly qualified trainees that fail to secure the necessary funds to begin an independent research career. According to reports from the NIH and the National Science Foundation (NSF), the number of biomedical research trainees that secure a fellowship grant to pursue an independent research career is less than 5% (Kolata, 2016). But it is also important to note that this is a fraction of the number of individuals that are capable of securing an academic research position. According to the NIH, only 25% of the number of trainees that obtain a biomedical research doctorate degree, are able to transition into an academic position (WGDBRW, 2012). The timeline increases for those individuals hoping to obtain their first career-award.

The problematic situation that has developed in biomedical research training and education, has not gone unnoticed, but the implementation of recommendations has not been fully engaged. Alberts and Rodgers (Alberts, 2014; Alberts, 2015; Rodgers, 2013) have developed key recommendations to improve the quality of biomedical research education, as well as to address the workforce development for those individuals that do pursue biomedical training. Some of these recommendations include: (1) The education of graduate students in the rigor of taking biomedical research training. (2)

Broadening the career paths of young scientists, including addressing the opportunities to seek training in other areas besides the lab. (3) Training of postdoctoral fellows, and effectively limiting the period of training to encourage advancement. (4) Using staff scientists, to effectively improve work quality and compensation. (5) Improving goals and mechanisms for scientific grants by essentially recognizing originality and goals, as well as providing resources to improve rewrites. (6) Improving evaluation criteria and the peer review process. (7) Strengthening grant panels by recruiting scientists to review. (8) Evaluating policies, programs and implementation. Even when the best policies and processes are developed, require follow-up evaluation to assess the success and failure in the execution of such work. In executing these recommendations, advisory committees can be beneficial in providing execution and assessment of new methods.

In all this, the lost concept is the outdated methods and techniques to continue to provide guidance and training to the new cohorts of graduate and postdoctoral trainees. Although the science has advanced, the instrumentation to carry out experiments has improved, and the knowledge has expanded, the same structure in developing advisory committees to guide biomedical research has remained unchanged. This leaves at odds a large number of highly qualified and trained individuals to squander for opportunities outside of the so-called ivory tower. It is important to note as well, that there is a number of trainees that after an intense training period, reflect that their professional interests are outside the academic environment (Lovits, 2001). In addition, a large number of highly trained and qualified individuals often seek opportunities outside the academic ivory tower. In order to address a number of issues associated with the different opportunities, challenges, reservations, beseeched in the biomedical research education and training, it is imperative to form advisory committees in biomedical research training. These advisory committees mush reflect the understanding of the large need to continue to cultivate and train a supply of biomedical research trainees needed to advance projects and improve health outcomes needed in biomedical research training. Conversely, advisory committees must also understand and assess the problems with 'alternative careers' for individuals who fail to continue a career in academia by securing independent research funds. The so called 'alternative careers' in biomedical research has been increasingly popular, but this more often has become the standard career for those that have advanced in a field aimed to continuing and producing in the academic setting (Finegold, 2005; Freedman, 2009; Mintz, 2010). The issue has never been to clear as it has been most recent. That the number of individuals seeking training in the biomedical research field is too vast to be able to secure the open opportunities in the academic setting.

A number of issues that have risen about the lack of academic positions, the weaning interest in academic research, and the lagging opportunities of research funding have been captured in a number of books, now helping trainees find opportunities to apply their talents and training outside biomedical research. However, a bigger issue is that even after an extremely demanding period of training, it seems that many highly trained biomedical research scientists often see their education as limiting to effectively and expediently begin contributing to the workforce. In biomedical research education and training, the time spent at the bench for trainees, often does not translate to development of skills that can be applied to other fields. Advisory committees can help trainees uncover new ways in which their training can fundamentally be applied in other areas outside the biomedical field.

Well-developed, diverse and conscientious advisory committees can fundamentally employ a number of strategies in order to improve the type of educational training and required skills so that trainees in the biomedical research enterprise are not only able to become scientific investigators, but also during the course of their scientific training, they can master a number of additional, transferable skills that can allow them to appropriately manage additional employment opportunities, especially when these may involve skills that are not directly related to laboratory skills.

The distinct difference between the training phase for vocational training between community college and a biomedical research education is remarkably interesting and vastly different. Community colleges have the ability to offer training with reduced costs and in time frames that consists of 24-36 months. Many of these training specifications and timeframes are necessary because this level of training education also takes resources from investing business that rely in dividends being brought back to their own business. In essence, collaborating business want a return on their investment to fund courses, equipment, and additional necessary expenses. Although community colleges can also apply for federal grants, these are often delegated to smaller institutions. Instead, much of the financial support is raised within the community and non-research grant funding.

Opposite to this is the overwhelming need for biomedical research institutions to secure federal funding as well as private grants that will support a different number of labs. Under this condition, it is up to the primary research investigator, who is the person responsible with securing funding sources in order to continue carrying out their proposed research and develop their area of expertise. Universities and institutions often secure the most desired investigators by luring them with attractive start-up packages. To continue the funding in training individuals in the biomedical research enterprise an institution may rely on a number of funding sources including, but not limited to: Federal funding, tuition funds from undergraduate education, trainees' own ability to secure trainee grants. Biomedical research education and training heavily relies on trainees working while completing their education. In return, the trainees receive a modest stipend.

A number of initiatives taken by the National Institutes of Health since 2015 seek to improve the development of the biomedical workforce and to accommodate the biomedical research and education in a number of areas that reflect the value of pursuing a biomedical research career.

UNDERSTANDING THE VALUE OF BIOMEDICAL RESEARCH

In order to understand the value of biomedical research (VOBR), it is critical to note that without the number of trainees pursuing this type of education that presents high value to a number of projects and discoveries that are essential to the advancement of new therapies, protocols, and interventions, to improve health outcomes, the biomedical field would not be at the advanced stage that is currently supported. Outbreaks are still critical problem that affects a number of underdeveloped countries, and that in developed nations it is a reality that with the increased expedience and ease of travel, such disease can quickly spread (Fauci, 1998).

Compared to a number of other fields, biomedical research training and education allows institutions to support a number of individuals through a vigorous period of scientific scholarship. Institutions are independent in a number of choices to accommodate the scientific training to those individuals seeking an education in biomedical research training, however there are a number of federal funding fellowships that encourage, and oftentimes require that appropriate training be given to those seeding biomedical research and training education. The goal is to ensure that the future of the biomedical research in the United States remains competitive and innovative. To this end, the National Institutes of Health has developed an advisory committee to the director to develop a model of recommendations that will appropriately continue to supply the quality and quantity of research trainees needed to advance projects and study assess new developments.

As mentioned in the previous chapter, the development of a biomedical research workforce has been created to improve participation of underrepresented minorities, however, additional working groups and advisory committees have similar tasks in improving workforce opportunities in additional populations. The Scientific Management Review Board, was tasked with developing a model for a sustainable and diverse U.S. biomedical research workforce that can inform decisions about training the optimal number of people for the appropriate types of positions that will advance science and promote health (SMRB, 2014). Based on this analysis and recognizing that there are limits to NIH's ability to control aspects of the training pipeline, the working group was asked to make recommendations for actions that NIH should take to support a future sustainable biomedical research infrastructure. The working group met 11 times in 2011 and 2012, including 4 in-person meetings and 7 teleconferences, with a goal to provide recommendations to the ACD in June 2012. In addition, a subcommittee consisting of social scientists (primarily economists) with expertise in the scientific enterprise and NIH-funded investigators with expertise in mathematical models was formed to gather and analyze data on the biomedical research workforce and develop a model. This report summarizes the workforce data collected and the working group's recommendations. The working group did not have either the time or the expertise to propose details on how the recommendations should be implemented. This will require thoughtful consideration by NIH. The working group recommends that changes to existing programs be phased in gradually and pilot programs be conducted to test new ideas. The outcomes of all changes should be evaluated rigorously (WGDBRW, 2012).

Another area in assessing the VOBR, is in terms of the impact in globalization. Although the United States continues to lead in research and development expenditures, and continues to deliver innovations to improve the biomedical research enterprise, there are a number of changing trends that can diminish the impact of the U.S. as the leader in this area (Conte, 2017). The amount in investment a country provides in research and development as part of its Gross Domestic Product is a good indicator of the economic health of that nation, and it recent years, the United States has undermined its leadership by severely cutting the funds it provides for biomedical research (Kristiansen, 2014). The global trends have now convincingly assert that other Asian nations, specifically Japan and China, have increased the percentage in research and development expenditures that can compete with the innovations developed in the United States (Chakma, 2014). In addition, this discourse can also result in decreasing the ability to import scientific talent to advance the American biomedical research enterprise. In stark contrast, nations that cannot yet compete with the United States in biomedical research, are reaching out efforts to collaborate with foreign biomedical agencies to improve the leadership and develop growth in biomedical research (Kay, 2015).

Development of partnerships, and cross-disciplinary collaboration is essential to not only increase the value of biomedical research, but also to translate the importance of its value. Involvement with the general public, as well as with policy makers can also increase the understanding of biomedical research in the United States (Steinbrook, 2004; Pramesh, 2016).

SUPPORTING THE BIOMEDICAL RESEARCH WORKFORCE

To ensuring the future of U.S. competitiveness and innovation in biomedical research is of utmost importance to the National Institutes of Health (NIH). One avenue for achieving this goal is to support a sustainable and diverse biomedical workforce. The results and recommendations for the working group of the Advisory Committee to the Director (ACD) stipulated major conclusions to improve workforce development.

The working group's analysis led to two major conclusions:

- The large upsurge in U.S.-trained Ph.D.'s, increasing influx of foreign-trained Ph.D.'s, and aging of the academic biomedical research workforce make launching a traditional independent academic research career increasingly difficult.
- The long training time, combined with the relatively low salaries for early career scientists when compared to other scientific disciplines and professional careers, may make a biomedical research career seem less attractive to the best and brightest of our young people.

NIH has undertaken the following initiatives to make progress towards achieving these goals between now and 2015:

1. Establish a grant program to encourage innovative training approaches.
2. Improve graduate student and postdoctoral researcher training.
3. Develop a simple and comprehensive tracking systems for trainees.

4. Encourage fair consideration of staff scientists on grant applications.
5. Initiate discussion with the community to assess NIH support of faculty.
6. Create an office in the NIH Office of the Director to assess the biomedical research workforce.
7. Conduct ACD Working Group study on optimal research training of individuals in clinical disciplines.

Additionally, a number of committees have developed to improve the best practices of research universities, as well as to ensure the continuity of the biomedical research workforce provided at member institutions of this committee (CCNIP, CRUNRC, RUFC). The work of these committees identifies areas for pursing challenging innovative ideas, seeking trends in global innovation, developing partnerships between research universities, national laboratories, and the private sector. It is important to note that these collaborations not only create an environment for fast innovation, but also improves funding opportunities, especially financial support from the largest public and philanthropic groups (Viergever, 2016).

ASSESSING THE VALUE OF BIOMEDICAL RESEARCH EDUCATION AND TRAINING FOR WORKFORCE DEVELOPMENT

The value of biomedical research extends to a number of areas that affect a variety of aspects in several differing industries. In 2006, the NIH developed a Scientific Management Review Board (SMRB) tasked with the opportunity to develop and identify appropriate parameters and approaches to assess and communicate the value of biomedical research (VOBR)(SMRB, 2014). In doing so it appropriately justifies the yearly funding expenses by the NIH, as well as identifies areas that will improve future appropriation of funding and develop guidelines to improve biomedical research. Task groups, or committees such as the scientific management review board, also dispel information that are emphatically relevant to the institutions receiving research grant funds directly from the NIH. The opportunity to obtain information and develop guidelines starting at an NIH-level task group and trickling down to individual institutions advisory committees strengthens the educational and training component for trainees. This also presents an opportunity to advance the effects that an advisory committee in biomedical research education and training presents in this field. The NIH working group continues to assess the variety of methods to improve the impact and quantification in the value of biomedical research, and from these, a number of recommendations can be implied and implemented so as to take value in development of free standing advisory committees in biomedical research to improve training and workforce transition in the biomedical research field. Some of these recommendations that best reflect effective use in advisory committees include:

1. Systematically, comprehensively and strategically assess the value of biomedical research for accountability, effective management and public awareness.
2. NIH's development of connections between generation of basic and clinical knowledge and the impact of this knowledge to enter translational pathways.
3. Assessment of NIH in the VOBR done in partnership with relevant stakeholders.
4. Development of trans-committees on assessment that will develop strategies to support assessments of value, determine strategic processes in selecting study topics, identification of promising analytical approaches to capture value and seek input from external expert.

The aforementioned strategies can be methodically and systematically applied to advisory committees in biomedical research to increment the impact and assessment of biomedical research at an institutional level. In addition, utilizing external partnerships to conduct assessments insures objectivity and effectiveness.

The National Institutes of Health, is the single most public funder of biomedical research in the world, with a variety of mechanisms to a number of institutional medical centers and universities. The NIH's nearly $31 billion budget in fiscal year 2012 supported approximately 50,000 competitive grants to more than 300,000 researchers at more than 2,000 US universities, medical schools and other research institutions in every state ad around the world. To this the impact of NIH funding also reaches over 1,200 principal investigators and 6,000 trainees. Undoubtedly, the large impact in funding from the NIH, and discerning the value of biomedical research is consequentially important, and the capture of value in biomedical research at its core requires the scientific knowledge, unwavering expertise and influence of a number of participants in the scientific and health enterprise.

The most affected group of individuals that provide increasing output based on their training and low-cost are postdoctoral fellow. This group of individuals provide an exceeding value to operate the biomedical research enterprise simply because although they provide knowledge and are highly trained, they continue to operate under a training environment and are compensated based on NIH guidelines. The population of postdoctoral fellows however, has steadily declined from 2010, and the number of trainees that choose to continue a postdoctoral training fellowship continues to decline (Garrison, 2016). The consequences of this, is that it may take a longer period of time to find discoveries when there is no expertise that is provided by postdoctoral fellows, as well as the potential decrease in the purchasing power of research grants if less postdoctoral fellows decide to avoid additional training because the compensation and benefits are not in line with what they may receive in other fields. Rather than staffing research laboratories with trainees, both graduate and postdoctoral, who are being prepared for a faculty position that may not materialize, consideration should be given to creating staff scientist positions that would also reflect a more attractive and adequate compensation (Gerbi, 2001).

The NIH serves as a steward of public funds to maintain responsible and effective use of resources. These resources have as its ultimate goal to address the health challenges that are faced nationally and globally. It is through a rigorous decision-making process that relies heavily on scientific expertise, and evidence-based stakeholder input to review, and determine the proposed projects and setting research and scientific priorities. In addition, a number of groups and academic advisory committees are taking initiatives to improve the workforce development not just for individuals that acquire highly specialized training in the biomedical field, but those that receive training in engineering, the physical, chemical, biological and social sciences. In *Rising Above the Gathering Storm*, (Members of the 2005 Committee), the members of the 2005 National Academies Committee discuss the pressing need to continue addressing the advocacy for the scientific research enterprise, this done as to ensure economic well-being, assist in the creation of new industries, promote public health, and to improve and care for the environment. In addition, individual institutions are staring to develop advisory committees to support entrepreneurship, commercialization, innovation, funding and trainee (PhD and postdoctoral fellow) career development in this arenas (CBSW).

In addressing the current recommendations to the value of biomedical research, it is important to extrapolate these to address workforce development. Diversity and continual input and recommendations from stakeholder entities will improve the outcomes and expected returns in job development in many areas not directly influenced by biomedical research, but that can utilize some of those individuals trained as research scientists.

THE REACH OF ADVISORY COMMITTEES

It is important to understand the reach of advisory committees under specific circumstances and within a place, institution, environment, industry, etc. In a complex and changing industrial world, advisory committees are essential to the development, planning and operations of a setting. In community college, advisory committees illustrate the sound performance of a vocational-technical educational program. In biomedical research and training, the same characteristic argument can be made. Biomedical research advisory committees are given the tasks of developing sound performance of an incrementally complex program that should cultivate the vocational and technical professionalism to advance health understanding and outcomes.

Regardless of the environment, advisory committees are fundamental in planning and operating vocational/technical education programs. In a community college setting, advisory committees are essential in developing tasks that test their depth in effecting positive outcomes. There is also a specific type of advisory committee, and these can also show relevance at the biomedical research level. A first type to be discussed is the advisory committee as a general committee. The general committee serves to review an occupational education program and present advice on additional immediate needs and foresee future one as financial outcomes change, funding mechanisms deter, and even if those funding mechanisms improve. In community college, this is especially important because the surrounding community is immediately affected by the number of individuals receiving specific training, as well as the advisory committee must assess the educational program to account for new technologies, changing trends and funding to continue programs. In biomedical research, because there is a large institution at hand providing the training, there is also a community element to the immediate economic health. However, biomedical research as a whole is much less affected by community industrial effects. Because biomedical research is largely funded by federal grants and private industrial venues, and because large institutions rely on additional educational training, mainly at the university level, there is not an immediate effect of the community in changing biomedical research programs. General advisory committees in biomedical research still play a role in looking at larger aspects and trends in the biomedical research field that would destabilize the status quo and would require modification in the programs and venues.

As for example, the University of Texas Medical Branch in Galveston Texas is an institution that is heavily influenced by the changing trends in threads posed to society by new and emerging diseases (utmb.edu). Some of which can be natural and some that can have man made origins. The University of Texas Medical Branch was then able to assemble a group that reflects the expertise, builds teams and creates strong programs of study and focus to learn to address the issues that threaten the entire communities and present a global health threats. UTMB has been organized under the Center of Biodefense and Emerging Infectious Diseases in order to lead programs and research to better understand the biological threats, and develop treatments and vaccines.

Today, the University of Texas Medical Branch in Galveston is not only a training ground in biomedical research, but it also employs a number of trained individuals in order to tackle some of the most pressing infectious diseases that remain a major cause of morbidity and mortality worldwide. Though it is still most commonly seen that these burden of infectious diseases falls most heavily on individuals in developing countries (African and South America for examples), citizens of industrialized countries are increasingly experiencing the effects, especially as international travel increases contact with the causative organisms.

Some of the emerging spread of emerging infectious diseases includes HIV/AIDS, Ebola, Zika, SARS/MERS, West Nile, and chikungunya, as well as other reemerging ones such as cholera, tuberculosis, scrub typhus, rabies and dengue. A number of investigators and funding agencies collaborate to increase the funding opportunities at institutions like UTMB, however, the constant reassessment by advisory committees categorically, methodically and expediently assess the needs that will establish training programs and specific biomedical workforce opportunities.

CONCLUSION

It is important to develop a model to sustain and diverse medical research workforce that can inform decisions about training. From the number of people that should be selected year after year for training opportunities, to the types of positions that will be able to improve and advance science to promote health. Advisory Committees serve well in developing these models, reach assessments, and implement recommendations. The analysis from such committees will often convey information to understand the consequences of the current policies and the recommendations to improve outcomes. In biomedical research, advisory committees serve numerous purposes. From developing a training curriculum, to the assessment of present and future needs in the academic research arena that also looks at the future needs in the industrial and academic setting. Additional components that where not expanded in this version of this script, is the impact on scientific policy, communication, and entrepreneurship. Additional issues that were also omitted, were the impact of the international community in biomedical research and training and the assessments that may be reached by advisory committees. Any future research into advisory committees in biomedical research training and education, should additionally include further assessment of current and future availability of trainees from the domestic and international communities.

Advisory committees continue to be implemented to guide a number of areas in community college education and training, and it could be assumed that the resources are respectably lesser than those available to four-year and additional biomedical research institutions and medical centers. It is then worthwhile that these institutions seek ways to form partnerships with interested community leaders. This will not only improve the outreach of universities and research institutions, but will also provide an opportunity for graduate researches exercise additional skills not often applied during their time in the lab.

From the number of people that should be selected year after year for training opportunities, to the types of positions that will be able to improve and advance science to promote health. Advisory Committees serve well in developing these models, reach assessments, and implement recommendations. The analysis from such committees will often convey information to understand the consequences of the current policies and the recommendations to improve outcomes. In biomedical research, advisory committees serve numerous purposes. From developing a training curriculum, to the assessment of present and future needs in the academic research arena that also looks at the future needs in the industrial and academic setting. Additional components that where not expanded in this version of this script, is the impact on scientific policy, communication, and entrepreneurship. Additional issues that were also omitted, were the impact of the international community in biomedical research and training and the assessments that may be reached by advisory committees. Any future research into advisory committees in biomedical research training and education, should additionally include further assessment of current and future availability of trainees from the domestic and international communities.

REFERENCES

Alberts, B., Kirschner, M. W., Tilghman, S., & Varmus, H. (2014). Rescuing US biomedical research from its systemic flaws. *Proceedings of the National Academies of Science., 111*(14), 5773–5777. doi:10.1073/pnas.1404402111 PMID:24733905

Alberts, B., Kirschner, M. W., Tilghman, S., & Varmus, H. (2015). Addressing systemic problems in the biomedical research enterprise. *Proceedings of the National Academies of Science., 112*(7), 1912–1913. doi:10.1073/pnas.1500969112 PMID:25691698

Chakma, J., Sun, G. H., Steinberg, J. D., Sammut, S. M., & Jagsi, R. (2014). Asias Ascent – Global trends in biomedical R&D expenditures. *The New England Journal of Medicine, 370*(1), 3–6. doi:10.1056/NEJMp1311068 PMID:24382062

Committee on Biomedical Scientific Workforce (CBSW), Johns Hopkins University, Office of the Provost. (n. d.). Initiatives. Retrieved from http://web.jhu.edu/administration/provost/initiatives/Committee on_the_Biomedical_Scientific_Workforce/index.html

Committee on Comparative National Innovation Policies. Best practice for the 21st century, National Research Council (CCNIP). (2012). Rising to the Challenge: U.S. Innovation Policy for the Global Economy. National Academies Press. Washington, D.C.

Committee on Research Universities, National Research Council. (CRUNRC). (2012) Research Universities and the Future of America: Ten Breakthrough Actions Vital to Our Nation's Prosperity and Security. National Academies Press. Washington D.C.

Conte, M. L. (2017). Globalization and changing trends of biomedical research output. *Journal of Clinical Investigation Insight.*

Fauci, A. S. (1998). New and reemerging diseases: The Importance of Biomedical Research. *Emerging Infectious Diseases*, *4*(3), 374–378. doi:10.3201/eid0403.980308 PMID:9716949

Finegold, D. (2005). Alternative Career options in the biomedical industry: The professional science master's degree. *Nature Biotechnology*, *23*(4), 503–504. doi:10.1038/nbt0405-503 PMID:15815680

Freedman, T. (2009). *Career Opportunities in Biotechnology and Drug Development* (1st ed.). Cold Spring Harbor Laboratory Press.

Gerbi, S. A., Garrison, H. H., & Perkins, J. P. (2001). Education. Workforce alternatives to graduate students? *Science*, *292*(5521), 1489–1490. doi:10.1126/science.1059268 PMID:11379627

Kay, S. (2015). Africa's leadership in biomedical research: Shifting the center of gravity. *Science Translational Medicine*, *7*(314), 1–3. doi:10.1126/scitranslmed.aad5529 PMID:26582894

Kolata, G. (2016) Lost in Academia: So Many Research Scientists, So Few Openings as Professors. *New York Times*. Retrieved from https://www.nytimes.com/2016/07/14/upshot/so-many-research-scientists-so-few-openings-as-professors.html

Kristiansen, C. (2014) America is losing biomedical research leadership to Asia. *Fogarty International Center.* Retrieved from https://www.fic.nih.gov/News/GlobalHealthMatters/january-february-2014/Pages/spending-investment-biomedical-research-development.aspx

Lovits, B. (2001). *Leaving the Ivory Tower: The Causes and Consequences of Departure from Doctoral Study*. Rowman & Littlefield.

Members of the 2005 "Rising Above the Gathering Storm" Committee. (2010). *Rising Above the Gathering Storm, Revisited: Rapidly Approaching Category 5*. Washington D.C.: National Academies Press.

Mintz, C. S. (2010). Non-traditional Career Options for Life Scientists. *ASBMB today*. Retrieved from http://www.asbmb.org/asbmbtoday/asbmbtoday_article.aspx?id=7868

Pramesh, C. S., Venkataramanan, R., Suvarna, V., Goel, N. S., Lakshman, S., Venkatesh, V., & Badwe, R. et al. (2016). Involvement of general public in biomedical research. *Perspectives in Clinical Research.*, *7*(4), 152–155. doi:10.4103/2229-3485.192029 PMID:27843788

Rodgers, B. D. (2013). When is education a disservice? *The FASEB Journal*, *27*(12), 4678–4681. doi:10.1096/fj.13-235762 PMID:23975933

Scientific Management Review Board (SMRB). (2014). Draft Report on approaches to assess the Value of Biomedical Research Supported by NIH. Retrieved from: https://smrb.od.nih.gov/documents/reports/VOBR%20 SMRB__Report_2014.pdf

Steinbrook, R. (2004). Science, Politics and Federal Advisory Committees. *The New England Journal of Medicine*, *350*(14), 1454–1460. doi:10.1056/NEJMhpr033416 PMID:15070798

The Research Universities Futures Consortium (RUFC). (2012). *The Current Health and Future Well-Being of the American Research University*. Philadelphia, PA: Elsevier.

Viergever, R. F., & Hendriks, T. C. C. (2016). The 10 largest public and philanthropic funders of health research in the world: What they fund and how they distribute their funds. *Health Research Policy and Systems*, *14*(1), 12. doi:10.1186/s12961-015-0074-z PMID:26892771

Working Group on the Diversity in the Biomedical Research Workforce (WGDBRW) and The Advisory Committee to the Director. (2012). Draft Report of the Advisory Committee to the Director Working Group on Diversity in the Biomedical Research Workforce. Retrieved from https://acd.od.nih.gov/documents/reports/DiversityBiomedicalResearchWorkforceReport.pdf

Chapter 6
Challenges to Working Collaboratively

Julie Neal
Independent Researcher, USA

ABSTRACT

It is important to gain perspective directly from business and industry, and the service providers through their own words and experiences, to create a complete outlook regarding the project and program under consideration. The discussion in this chapter is the result of the research findings gained in 2015 by interviewing workforce practitioners in the areas of welding, auto mechanics, criminal justice, information technology, surveying, diesel technology, and applied technology. The chapter includes discussions from practitioners regarding: decision-making process, lack of knowledge, effects of business and industry on workforce programs, advisory committees, and best practices—a unique discussion offered by practitioners with years of experience, all of whom serve on advisory committees.

INTRODUCTION

This chapter has been added for the reader to get a first-hand account of what individuals currently working with advisory committees have experienced and the lessons learned from those accounts. The following is only a portion of the dissertation filed in 2015 that has been included to give the reader a clearer picture of what advisory committees are and how they function. Mainly included are the findings and recommendations from the participants.

DOI: 10.4018/978-1-5225-4083-0.ch006

Of specific foci that are added to this discussion are the decision-making processes and the strategies used by stakeholders that readers may be able to incorporate within their own institutions.

The purpose of this study was to explore perceptions of and experiences with advisory committees that community-college practitioners and workforce-education programs utilize. It focused on the specific decision-making processes and the strategies perceived to be best practices for enhancing collaboration among stakeholders. This study will contribute to the practice of higher education, and the body of knowledge used by community-college workforce advisory committee members to make informed decisions for workforce-education programs.

The participants were asked to focus on four specific questions that guided this study:

1. What do community-college practitioners and advisory-committee members perceive are effective practices and strategies in the decision-making process related to workforce programs?
2. What do community-college practitioners and advisory-committee members perceive as challenges to working collaboratively?
3. How do community-college practitioners and advisory committee members perceive the decision-making process of business and industry impacting the decisions made for workforce-education programs?
4. What recommendations do community-college practitioners and advisory-committee members have for collaborative decision-making?

The boundaries of this study were set by focusing on two community colleges located in the South Plains region of Texas. The participants included those involved in workforce-education programs at the two institutions, either as department chairpersons of a workforce program, or advisory members from business and industry. The inclusion criteria for the college participants were that they took part in programs that used advisory committees to make informed decisions for workforce programs; and that they had been employed within the community-college system in a workforce program in Texas for at least two years. This requirement ensured that the college participants possessed a strong background and familiarity with advisory committees and workforce-program requirements within the state of Texas. The second group was advisory member participants. The inclusion criterion for them was that they were currently serving or had served on an advisory committee at one of the study institutions within the past two years (at the time of this study). The two institutions in this study were rural-serving, medium-sized West Texas public community colleges, located in the South Plains region of Texas. Participants and institution names were not used in the study, and will not be identified here.

DECISION-MAKING PROCESS

All participants agreed that decision-making was one of the most difficult tasks in their roles on the committee. One advisory member participant stated, "Being on the advisory committee, you have to know what to ask, how to ask it, and assess what the actual needs are in a community—this is decision-making." Even though all advisory members agreed that decision-making for an entity was difficult, they possessed the confidence to make decisions for the college, because of their years of experience and proven track records. A community-college department-chair participant explained, "Decision-making is something that comes with experience and time." He went on to say, "We don't want all yes people on our committees—questioning keeps us focused and accountable for the decisions made in committee and the impact of those decisions."

Advisory committees are familiar with identifying program/project needs, ascertaining feasible and effective solutions, and generating public interest and funding for the projects/programs. All of the advisory member participants discussed how proud they were to be on the advisory committee for the college program, putting as much into the decision-making at these meetings as they did at their own businesses. One advisory member participant shared that "the decisions we make are not just building for tomorrow, but we are building for the next generation by managing for the good times to take care of the down times." The members expressed ownership and pride that bind and create rapport for a successful working relationship. Participants agreed that workforce programs should be built around values, professionalism, and ethics; and that the advisory committee members should use these values and expectations to make decisions for the program. Many of the participants discussed how the advisory committee represents them as business/industry in the community, and how the decisions they make reflect on their personal businesses. Including members who take ownership in the committee connects them directly with their own business.

Workforce programs require a decisive and productive decision-making process that is key to successful practices and strategies. Including individuals on the committee who are confident, skilled, experienced in making decisions, weigh their options, voice opinions, and genuinely care about the program is optimal for program success. Dougherty (2015) and DiMattina (2014) claim the same of individuals who not only care about the product they are producing, the educational involvement, and future employees, but also have connections to the community they serve. Members skilled at communicating with both business/industry and the college work collaboratively, and are key to establishing successful practices and strategies for workforce-education programs. The advisory committee combines experts in the area of study, including administrators, financial backers, and influential members within the local communities, helping to ensure significant business and industry input.

The findings of this study reveal that advisory committees consist of a group of diverse business and industry decision-makers who use their experiences to help with the decision-making process of the committee. Because the decisions an advisory committee makes are complex, adding multiple perspectives allows the committee to assess the probable success of a workforce-education program with input from experts in the field of study (Allingham, 2002; Burke & Miller, 1999). The research reveals that the findings in this area are similar to the work of Kilcrease (2011), who states that an advisory committee has more success when various specialties and occupations of expertise are represented. As identified in the GIPWE (2015), successful advisory committees generally consist of influential individuals who generate public support for the workforce programs. The department-chair participants shared that business and industry advisory-committee members are aware of current trends, modern changes, and advancements in workforce programs, and are willing to share their knowledge with members of the advisory committee. The research of Kilcrease (2011) supports these findings by confirming that leaders of business and industry working collaboratively with college leaders, using honed decision-making skills, is beneficial when unexpected challenges arise. The consistently changing demands of business and industry complicate the decision-making process for workforce programs (Day, 2001; Kilcrease, 2011).

Therefore, the workforce advisory committee must include proven decision-makers from business and industry, who have the ability to combine company decisions with the college's vision. The college is committed to its vision and mission, and employees support that vision (Sena, Sena, & Crable, 2010). The advisory committee's function is to make decisions in the best interest of the college. Mintzberg (1979) defines decision-making as "the process of developing a commitment to a course of action" (p. 58). This definition supports the processes that advisory committees use in making the best decisions for workforce programs. The word "commitment" reflects the significance of advisory members following through on the decisions made while in committee, and completing the course of action as discussed.

LACK OF KNOWLEDGE REGARDING EDUCATIONAL SYSTEM

A major theme emerged from the research, regarding the challenges that community colleges face when trying to work collaboratively with business and industry, insofar as community colleges differ from business and industry. They do not just specialize and focus on one particular educational area; education represents many diverse programs. Business and industry traditionally specialize in one product, and that is the area of their expertise. This creates a challenge for community colleges, because they need a diverse set of experts in order to have a voice representing areas the program embodies. This challenge can be addressed through the advisory committee acting as the liaison and link between the college's workforce-education program and the community (Davis & Davis, 2009; Kerka, 2002; Kilcrease, 2011). The operations of a community college may differ from business and industry, but the decision-making talents of many individuals (Jones, 2006; Spector, 2012) on the advisory committee result in an effective workforce-education program.

Advisory member participants also addressed a lack of understanding of the community-college rules. The members acknowledged this inhibits the committee's ability to help the college excel to its fullest potential by using the rules to the advisory committee's advantage. Two of the department-chair participants shared that the advisory committee normally accepts what the college reports regarding the rules. The participants noted that as members get tenure on the committee, their knowledge increases about the rules and regulations that govern community colleges. This increased understanding provides a knowledge base that the committee can use to function more productively within those guidelines. Findings by Meeder and Pawlowski (2012) support the perceptions of the participants in this study—namely, that business and industry are familiar with working within government regulations and finding ways to excel. This knowledge and understanding within the committee environment is important to members making informed decisions, and not becoming frustrated with rules they do not understand.

HIRING EMPLOYEES AND COMPLETERS

Department-chair participants noted that students in internships want to accept employment before finishing their studies. However, the participants stated that this is not the best course of action for the student, the college, or the employer. A student who leaves the workforce program prior to completion risks failing to obtain credentials necessary for employment. In addition, students miss out on future courses that can enhance their knowledge and skills. Research conducted by Burke and Miller (1999) supports the contention that individuals who are willing to make concessions and negotiate best serve in the area of workforce-education programs. This statement would be true for business and industry, as well as for the student. The community college has streamlined current certificate programs to achieve stronger economic payoffs (Kazis, 2011). As the connection between business/industry and the college, the advisory committee can help address the issue of students leaving the college prior to the completion of the program. Since business and industry are providing the internships, having a prior agreement and understanding with employers can help solve this issue. Employers working with the advisory committee can encourage and make allowances for students so they can obtain their credentials by completing all training (Davis & Davis, 2009; Kilcrease, 2011). The advisory committee can work as a facilitator of internships for the student, and also help students locate gainful employment (Benigni, Ferguson, & McGee, 2011; Davis & Davis, 2009). The department-chair participants acknowledged that business and industry in their local communities are working with the college and the students to assist with tuition, modifying hours, and providing internships. The community realizes the importance of the programs, and is working with the students and the advisory committee in an effort to help ensure students complete their studies before obtaining full-time employment.

WORKFORCE RESPECT AND TRUST

As noted previously, the participants in this study perceive that workforce education programs should be built around values, professionalism, and ethics, to remain sustainable. Part of the collaboration between the college and business/industry is that all parties are involved in the entire process. The findings of this study indicate that the department-chair participants value the needs of all stakeholders in advisory-committee meetings, and encourage their participation; and stakeholders trust that the committee will listen as they present their needs. All participants commented that it does not do the community a service when the collaboration is only for name recognition, and not to truly work collaboratively to provide a united program for the community. According to advisory member participants and department-chair participants, this is an important step in proving to the community that everyone should respect and trust what the advisory committee is trying to do for the program it serves, and that it will not be fully productive without all stakeholders involved. Trust in the advisory committee must be established at the beginning; then the respect will follow, once the members realize they are working with professionals for the good of all, and not just for one company's special interest. The participants expressed that it is difficult to reinforce their appreciation of each member, but that this is a necessary component of showing to the community the value they hold for each member, the community, and the program.

A department-chair participant provided an inimitable finding concerning trust and respect, by explaining that his relationship of trust and respect with the community developed because of the years he spent working in his own shop with the same group of individuals. The literature supports the importance of an owner's relationship with the community by explaining that members who have influence within the local community are instrumental in seeking support for programs (e.g., Johnson, 2013). The department chair stated that he is always up front with individuals when asking for equipment or donations, and makes sure the advisory-committee members and the department know where the equipment will go, how it will be used, what benefits will come with it, and how the funds were being spent and why. The findings of this study reveal, through the perceptions of the participants, that trust and respect take time and are the key to seeking monetary help. The trust and respectful relationship that the workforce department chair has with the advisory-committee leader is vital for lobbying for money and equipment from within the community.

The final finding is relative to respect and trust for workforce-education programs in general. Advisory member participants expressed the sentiment that workforce education does not receive the same recognition as other academic disciplines. The advisory-committee participants articulated that the product being produced through workforce-education programs is vital to the economy and stability of a global workforce. Yet, the programs do not receive attention for their latest advancements and securing jobs for employees in the workforce, even though the literature fully supports that workforce-education training has a direct connection to improving the economy (e.g., Bray, 2011). Other scholars, including Bray (2011), recognize that workforce-education programs provide retraining to unemployed workers, resulting in a decreased unemployment rate and a boost to the economy (e.g., Hodges, 2012; Kazis, 2011). As research shows, business and industry working together with community colleges produces a skilled workforce, contributing to a decreased unemployment rate (e.g., Bray, 2011; Price & Roberts, 2009); yet little of this is advertised or distinguished. Since workforce education is relevant to an employable society, community colleges and advisory committees must publicly acknowledge and express their gratitude for the collaboration with business and industry and their contributions to the progress of the community, in order to help address the stigma surrounding employment in midlevel workforce positions.

EFFECTS OF BUSINESS AND INDUSTRY ON WORKFORCE PROGRAMS

The participants agreed that business/industry internships and the training received from the college prepare the students to be critical thinkers. Critical thinking is described as purposeful analysis; the ability to self-regulate and to discern and evaluate (Paul, 1994); well-thought-out process (Beyer, 1995); and gaining information by observation, experience, action, reflection, communication, and explanation (National Council for Excellence in Critical Thinking, 1987). All participants agreed that the hands-on internship experience helps match students by their ability, and creates the critical-thinking skills needed for employment. Specifically, students connect their formal classroom training with real- life experiences, and become lifelong critical thinkers. Research supports aligning job training with current economic workforce needs to develop a highly-qualified labor supply and a long-term supply of workers contributing to a strong, sustainable economy (e.g., Baber, 2011; Hodges, 2012; Kazis, 2011). Working directly with business and industry during the internship helps students know what to ask, how to ask, and how to probe for more answers. Students working hands-on and side-by-side, through internships with business and industry, creates performance-driven students. The student then has a toolbox of knowledge to ask relevant questions, seek answers, and produce quality products, with attention to detail using critical-thinking skills in the workforce.

Research conducted by Kazis (2011) supports producing graduates more quickly through the restructuring of programs and the internship, to help make critical thinkers of the students, with hands-on training that potential employers provide. The findings of the research support the work of Kazis—namely, the participants also perceived that advisory-committee member connections and their own companies create internships, playing an important role in the critical-thinking skills of students. The advisory committees help develop programs from start to finish. Placing students in internships creates a network connection with business and industry, as well as an opportunity for placement after completion of training. These findings align with the works of Johnson (2013) and Meeder and Pawlowski (2012), who find that advisory-committee members who have influence within the local community are influential in securing placement of students after they complete the program (Johnson, 2013). Using the community college's flexibility to quickly develop training programs to match workforce demands, especially in areas that lack skilled workers (Bray, 2011; Hodges, 2012), these internships provide opportunities for graduates' possible future employment. DiMattina (2014) confirms that community colleges have the ability to react to changes in industry quickly, and can offer degrees and certificates in specifically focused areas. According to Bray (2011), to meet the changing needs of a community, community colleges provide shortened workforce-education programs, including internships sponsored by the advisory-committee members and other community members. Employers are looking for employees who have the ability to think critically and find solutions using their workforce-education training and internship experience.

ADVISORY COMMITEES SET DIRECTION OF PROGRAMS

Business/industry and community colleges share a vision by looking toward the future of the services they provide. Since business and industry are opportunity driven, and focus on providing solutions, they watch for the next opportunity or evolving challenge. All of the research participants mentioned that both entities face many challenges. The guidance and leadership provided by business and industry allows community colleges to take advantage and try out new ideas to address changes and challenges, and then pass on what they have learned to the colleges. The decisions the advisory committee makes are complex, requiring the expertise of multiple members to help assess the probability of success of a workforce-education program (Allingham, 2002; Burke & Miller, 1999; Day, 2001). Day (2001) points out that if the general make-up of the advisory committee represents expertise in various specialties and occupations, the direction of the program will be successful. Similar to Day, but in a different context, the advisory-committee member participants noted that the challenges were especially poignant in the South Plains region of West Texas, where the study institutions are located. That area had experienced a surge (2011) in oil and gas production, a downturn (2014), and currently is back to another surge (2016), changing the immediate needs of the community. Through this challenge, business/industry has worked to gather the information to address challenges, and then passed it along to the advisory committees to set the direction. As a result, the direction and needs of the strong oil and gas community began to be addressed by business and industry, working with the community college to train employees for immediate needs. This collaboration became evident in the equipment and funds shared with the colleges, as well as in the expertise shared with the programs.

The community college is known for running efficient and streamlined programs that fit the needs of an emergent community. DiMattina (2014) previously identified findings similar to those found by this study. DiMattina found that business and industry working together with community colleges under the guidance of the department chair, through the workforce advisory committee, create community job training that can successfully train, demonstrate, negotiate, deliver, adjust, plan, and merge talents. Carlson et al. (2011) reveal that leaders who are familiar with the community, and have already established a relationship with stakeholders, are better prepared to guide the advisory-committee members toward making decisions regarding the best direction for the workforce program. This flexibility is needed during times of economic stress, due to the changes in workforce skill demands. The result is a trained workforce to accommodate the changing needs of the South Plains region of West Texas, where business/industry alone lacked the ability to train employees to adapt to a rapidly changing economy (AACC & National Center on Education and the Economy [NCEE], 2009; Kazis, 2011).

The findings in this study reveal that collaborations are imperative and supported by the ACT (2012), which projects that training in workforce career areas will account for 23% of all job openings between 2008 and 2018. Working with business and industry through the advisory committee will identify and target future employment opportunities. It is predicted that the labor demands are growing rapidly and community-college workforce programs are a vital necessity (ACT, 2012); they are a necessary component in higher education's connection to economic strength. The findings of this study continue to support that the advisory committee helps set the direction in which workforce programs will go in the future, as community colleges are tied to their mission statement and have the final say regarding any program changes, as regulated by state oversight boards. Because workforce programs increase and deepen the relationships between the college and the community, while also creating a vested interest among the local citizenry (Carlson, 2011), collaborations between the college and business/industry are vital, but must occur without the college losing its identity. As mentioned previously in this study, community colleges find themselves in a precarious situation as a result of continual budget constraints (Bray, 2011). The research produced by Jacobs (2014) confirms that workforce-education programs are more expensive to start up and maintain. As the findings in this study indicate, the department-chair participants agreed that their role as administrators often revolves around making decisions regarding program development. The research literature indicates that community colleges are offsetting the expenses associated with workforce-education programs by collaborating with local businesses and industries, and following through with their suggestions by using effective department chairs as liaisons (e.g., Carlson et al., 2011; Greenstone & Looney, 2011). The role of the department chair is more important than ever to securing and maintaining a collaborative environment that reflects the mission of the community college. The rapport and communication that department chairs establish with business and industry can lead to regularity of donations, equipment, internships, access to the latest information available, and a voice within the community.

ADVISORY COMMITTEES SUPPORT THE COLLEGE

All successful advisory committees possess a convincing, direct, take-charge personality that carries over to the advisory-committee meetings. The advisory-committee participants all had a strong connection and network within the community, and perceived the importance of giving back, which equates to soliciting donations to provide instructors and training equipment for the college. The committee members' connection to the college was evident in their discussions, as they described sharing their skills, donating their time, and pride in their affiliation with the college. Finding business/industry individuals who possess these qualities and have a true connection to the project is a major element of a successful advisory committee. Research conducted by DiMattina (2014) and Meeder and Pawlowski (2012) confirms that the support of these businesses and industries serves to promote effective community engagement, generate community interest, develop courses, recommend development of courses, identify business needs, secure corporate participation, and offer professional guidance to the college. Individual and financial support are both needed (Texas Workforce Commission, 2013). This point is supported by the National Center for Education Statistics ([NCES], 2010) and Soares (2010) when they suggest that business/industry leaders are willing to partner with community colleges and acknowledge their share of training expenses, as colleges are growing rapidly while their budgets are continuing to decrease.

Cohen, Brawer, and Kisker (2014) also suggest opening channels of communication to merge public and private funds, so that an equitable share is borne by each—business/industry and the community college. As noted by Carlson et al. (2011), the initial start-up of a program is costly without partnering with business and industry. All of the department-chair participants in this study agreed that individuals, who can explain to community leaders how working collaboratively to support the workforce program in turn supports their success as well, are crucial to forming effective advisory committees.

The findings confirm the sentiments stated by all the department-chair participants, with regard to the significance of state budget cuts to workforce-education programs. Oliff, Palacios, Johnson, and Leachman (2013) find that budget restrictions have consequences for colleges and their students. The continued budget cuts in higher education require colleges to cut faculty and programs, and raise tuition, which further burdens students with increased debts, and diminishes the quality of education (Oliff et al., 2013). Collaborations between community-college workforce programs and business/industry are a key component of keeping workforce programs funded, equipment and internships available, and community support intact. The advisory committee is central to such success (Meeder & Pawlowski, 2012).

The sentiments stated by all of the department chair participants in regard to the significance of state budget cuts to workforce education programs are confirmed in the findings. The studies conducted by Oliff, Palacios, Johnson, and Leachman (2013), who found that budget restrictions have consequences for colleges and their students. The continued budget cuts in higher education require colleges to cut faculty and programs, raise tuition which further burdens students with increased debts, and diminishes the quality of education (Oliff et al., 2013). The need for collaborations between community college workforce programs and business and industry is a key component in order to keep workforce programs funded, equipment and internships available, and supply community support -- the advisory committee is central to the success (Meeder & Pawlowski, 2012).

The community college budget may seem like an anomaly to business/industry that works on income, profit projections, and revenue. Since the Texas Higher Education Coordinating Board (THECB) is demanding more accountability and curriculum changes within the state of Texas (Oliff et al., 2013), the decision-making and support of business and industry, justifying changes and expenditures to stakeholders, are more important than ever. Decision-making is a process that will take time and groundwork the community college—especially the workforce department chair—sets down. Community-college department chairs deal with budget restrictions, and understand the vital importance of community connections to assist with program funding. Two department chairs expressed the realization that their department's financial success relies heavily on connections they make in the community, to secure equipment and funds for their programs. All of the department-chair participants exhibited strong and confident personalities, and had no reservations about calling on business and industry, as well as networking to make connections with local community individuals for support, important traits noted by DiMattina (2014).

Participants also pointed out that workforce department chairs that achieve a strong bond with an influential business/industry leader within the community are able to secure support, financing, equipment, and a connection to current product knowledge for their workforce-education program. The research of Meeder and Pawlowski (2012) reports that the trust and supportive relationship between the workforce department chair and business/industry leaders will impact the success of the workforce-education program and relationships with the community. As decision-making is a continual process, a balance between the workforce dean, department chair, and business/industry leaders is imperative for a successful and productive collaboration. It is important to take full advantage of the positive impact the relationship will yield over time, by including flexibility, willingness to negotiate, and setting the direction the committee will take into consideration.

BEST PRACTICES

An effective practice is including and working with the majority of businesses in the community, and making decisions based on equal representation of all community businesses, regardless of size. The advisory committee needs to open its platform to others, and find out what type of services it can provide for the community as a whole, not just those who attend meetings. If the advisory committee is to serve and represent the needs of the local community, it must find out exactly what those needs are, and then voice them to the committee that can act on them as a whole. An effective advisory committee represents the majority, and not just the few, when using best practices in its decision-making process, to produce an effective workforce program providing services for the entire community it serves.

Not all businesses operate using the same skill sets, and not all students are trained to provide services for just one type of operation. The college is matching the skills required within the community, and incorporating them into its program with the help of the advisory committee. Taking advantage of local community business/industry operators' knowledge in specific areas, these experts can analyze college programs, and make curriculum recommendations to boost a program or add and develop a new area. Advisory members have been known to share their specific curriculums and skill sets with the committee to provide input on the specific skill sets they are using, and allow the college to incorporate their requirements into their training. This allows a broader area of coverage for the student, equating to more marketability.

An advisory committee spearheads the decision-making process, engaging in the process from its inception, and continuing to be active and fluidly participate in the programs until they cease to exist. The role of the committee is ongoing and active throughout the duration of the program (Kerka, 2002).

The purpose of the advisory committee is to use result-driven practices to improve the prosperity of the project/program (AACC & NCEE, 2009; Kerka, 2002).

Discussing advisory committee obligations, local West Texas workforce department chairs expressed a strong community presence in the area their institutions serve, understanding that it is imperative for the college to work closely with businesses in town. In order to obtain a full perspective on the project at hand, small and large entities must be present and included on the committee, to prohibit one entity from becoming too influential. For example, if the college only has access to one type of welding machine, training students only for that particular type of welding limits the training for the students. An advisory-committee chair and members would approach welding facilities using alternative machine types, and request that they donate equipment to the facility, so the college may broaden the particular skill-set training it offers, and provide trained employees to the community. This type of broad training is advantageous to the students, as it provides a wider range of skills that can transfer to other areas, not just locally.

Practitioners who work in the field of welding encouraged balancing the committee by having a one-to-one balance of one welder for one applied-technology member. These individuals should be experts in their field and include current practitioners, because information is constantly changing and being updated. Sharing and informing the committee with regard to the latest and newest technology, techniques, and equipment available should be a continual process for the members. No committee members want to spend time hearing antiquated information. The majority of committee members will appreciate sharing and learning current and updated ideas, because they are in an ever-changing industry. In order for the collaborative decision-making initiatives to work, a committee working together could lead the way to train, demonstrate, negotiate, deliver, adjust, plan, and complete the merging of ideas, in an effort to disseminate effective practices and strategies.

WIDE RANGE OF ACTIVE COMMUNITY MEMBERS

Participants agreed collaborative decision-making should involve a wide range of community members. All department-chair participants identified the need for strong individuals from within the college and from business/industry, to solicit members of the community to give of their time, funds, and equipment to the program. Meeder and Pawlowski (2012) support having strong, vocal, and confident leadership on the advisory committee, which they perceive results in ownership of the workforce program, equating to success. Other research supports including individuals who have the ability and commitment to make decisions, and become committed to a course of action (e.g., Mintzberg, 1979). One advisory member participant shared that business and industry use tenacity, confidence, and perseverance to address challenges and employ a "never say never" attitude. For example, when her budget was cut one year, she reached out to the advisory members for key information on companies going out of business that might give or sell equipment and supplies to her program at reduced prices. The networking and leads she gained from her advisory committee opened doors for her to use her funds more efficiently, spending her limited budget in the most cost-effective way. This leadership style has transformed the advisory committee into a powerful asset, led by consultants and executives sharing their experiences with workforce programs at the community colleges. Previous literature supports including enthusiastic and committed members on the committee for the overall success of the workforce-education program (e.g., Johnson, 2013). Further, to create unity among the members, a strong leader will assist members of a committee to see the benefits associated with making concessions and negotiating, to best serve the needs of the workforce-education program (Burke & Miller, 1999; Johnson, 2013; Northouse, 2013).

The findings of this study support prior research that a specific criterion for advisory committee members depends heavily on the department chair's temperament, and especially the disposition of the department chair. The prior relationship the department chair has had with business/industry within the local community, prior to entering the community college workforce program, becomes an extension of the advisory committee (Sena et al., 2010). A department-chair participant stated that she includes individuals on the committee whom she knew from business, including professionals with whom she worked prior to working for the college. Including these individuals gave her the boost she needed, to get meetings going and help her make connections within the community.

DiMattina (2014) stresses that it is important for advisory committee members to be knowledgeable in the field in which they serve, as they represent the voice of their industry. Like Allingham (2002) Burke and Miller (2011) find that the complex decisions that colleges and business/industry make together require the perspectives and expertise of multiple members.

One advisory member participant stated that he finds it imperative to include members on the advisory committee who can be trusted, and who have an in-depth understanding of the needs of the program. He also said that he prefers "down to earth individuals that are considered blue-collar workers in town with a deep understanding in the field that will speak openly, be the voice of their industry, and community minded." The review of the literature for this study suggests that a progressive advisory committee should consist of individuals with varying leadership experiences and management styles (e.g., Dixon, 1990), with transparency in the decision-making process a critical element of the committee's success of (e.g., Bess & Dee, 2008), along with commitment to the process.

NETWORKING OPPORTUNITIES

Networking is an essential component of advisory committees and their meetings. A finding of this study that was common to all study participants was that most of the individuals on the committee use the meetings as an opportunity to connect with other business/industry leaders, to gain insight regarding changes in the industry. Prior research supports that this is a benefit to advisory committees, as it helps them create programs, obtain resources, and develop public awareness of training programs (e.g., GIPWE, 2015; THECB, 2013). The research of Day (2001) and Kilcrease (2011) is similar to the perceptions of some of the participants in this study, who state that having professionals from within the community on the committee helps guide workforce programs toward needed support.

The literature presented in this study supports the advantages of networking to advisory committees. Carlson et al. (2011) explain that business/industry leaders realize that combining efforts to train workers results in effective economic gain, through the sharing of materials, supplies, equipment, and services. Networking opportunities help business and industry align job training with current economic workforce needs, in order to generate a highly-qualified labor supply, specifically in middle-skill jobs; and contributes to a long-term supply of workers and a strong, sustainable economy (Baber, 2011; Hodges, 2012; Kazis, 2011). For community colleges to accomplish these goals, regional needs must be aligned with workforce needs, and the workforce-education program is designed to provide this needed training (Hodges, 2012; Perna, 2012).

President Barack Obama announced in 2009 the American Graduation Initiative (AGI) challenge to community colleges, to educate an additional five million students with credentials, certificates, and degrees by 2020. Networking between the community college and business/industry became more important than ever to accomplish this goal, because businesses and industry working with community colleges is part of an effort to put Americans back to work in needed skilled areas to help the economy (Carlson et al., 2011; Soares, 2010), and requires capitalizing on prior networking connections with other community members. Individual businesses and community colleges do not have the funds or skills necessary to train, conduct research, and market all of their needs, especially when competing globally (ACT, 2012; Carlson et al., 2011). But networking with other stakeholders through the workforce advisory-committee meetings helps to provide a platform to discuss and find solutions to achieve their goals.

HONESTY AND TRANSPARENCY

A majority of the participants addressed the need to be honest and transparent in advisory committee meetings and with advisory committee members. A department-chair participant noted that he is completely transparent with his advisory committee. Another department-chair participant perceived that transparency is of the utmost importance to the successful functioning of the advisory committee, in order to help the committee air out any issues and speak freely. Typically, this technique is used in business and industry meetings, but it is not often found in community-college meetings, which tend to be more structured. DiMattina (2014) comments that a heated discussion can lead to solving problems faster, and lets other advisory members know how important an issue is for a particular industry. Honesty and transparency among committee members reveal the underlying issues within the committee. The honest and transparent perspectives of multiple members are necessary to assess accurately the need and probable success of a workforce-education program (Allingham, 2002; Burke & Miller, 1999). Advisory committees generally consist of a variety of individuals with varying leadership management styles (Dixon, 1990); transparent decision-making is critical for group success (Bess & Dee, 2008).

VOICE OF THE COMMITTEE

Members represent the voice of the committee; therefore, it is important that the participants know their role and duty, as members of the advisory committee, to give accurate input and advice. The committee utilizes its expertise and industry skills to form recommendations in the field of education for accreditation, curriculum, adding and replacing classes, degree-plan changes, and program adjustments, in order for educational programs to best meet the needs of the college and the program. The biomedical committee utilizes a guiding principle of providing counsel, advice, collaboration, and assessment of research projects, by experts working directly in the field. The project chair ensures that all who may be affected by the offerings of the project being overseen are invited to meetings and included in the discussions. All participants have a role to play, and must speak up, sharing their input and professional experiences.

The advisory members act as the voice of the industry, and help set the skills needed for the program. In order for the college to adjust its program curriculum to community needs, business/industry must voice their concerns and needs to the committee, so they can contemplate and make informed decisions. This will give business and industry a chance to be vocal, express how the program is meeting competencies, and match the skills that are necessary for certification and employment. The decision-making process is crucial to creating sustainable economic growth within the advisory committee and the community. Collaborating with the community, workforce programs and business/industry align job training with economic requirements, resulting in trained, employable workers.

To achieve results-driven progress as a committee, a deep-rooted respect and trust must be established within the membership. The experience, expertise, and knowledge gained by the advisory committee members through personal experiences, including trial and error, results in their recommendations to the committee. Advisory-committee members are expected to offer professional advice and programmatic recommendations based on the needs of the local community and their professional experience (Collins Community College, 2011; LCC, 2013). Having advisory-committee members directly involved with business and industry on the committee gives them the opportunity to share current trends and needs with the committee, to advise and give direction for workforce programs. It is important that the committee be relevant, and recommend current and upcoming trends in the industry. Therefore, all members of the community, whom the decisions of the advisory committee may affect, must have a voice and be represented. Findings by Baber (2011), Bray (2011), and Kress (2012) support that colleges and business/industry must work collaboratively, in order to ensure that offered programs meet the needs of the workforce.

According to Soares (2010), the key to community colleges working collaboratively with business and industry is to include the right individuals on the advisory committee—those who are dedicated to not only their business, but to the college as well. Finding the right individuals for the committee requires including active members in the community, and those who know how the community operates on a daily basis. However, even though business and industry may be abundant in most communities, not all have successful decision-makers, and even fewer are willing or have time to invest with another organization (Kilcrease, 2011). Identifying community members who are willing to give back to their community by way of collaborating with their local community college and advisory committee may be a challenge. Community officials, chamber of commerce members, Rotary members, and long-standing residents within the community could address this issue. Influential advisory members have the ability to generate support for the local community-college workforce programs, and also offer relevant advice (Carlson et al., 2011; Soares, 2010). Members willing to pick up the phone, knock on doors, and use networking to find business and industry are also key to a successful workforce-education program. Of great importance to the success of the committee is finding a true leader within the community to head the advisory committee—one who is committed to the community and his or her business. The leader must want to represent the voice of the industry, and be able to see the bigger picture, especially with any challenges the community is experiencing, such as an economic downturn, or trying to meet emerging oil and gas industry demands. The advisory committee leader's role is to influence others to work toward a common goal, and not take on the project as his or her sole responsibility (e.g., Carson, Tesluk, & Marrone, 2011; Northouse, 2013). It should be noted that community-college administrators and personnel are not eligible to chair the committee, which GIPWE regulations point out. The relationship of the advisory committee is a reciprocal one, Business/industry members receive a limitless supply of skilled workers with the most recent training available, as provided by the collaborative efforts of the advisory committee. Business/industry keep the educational institutions informed of coming advances in the industry, and any information able to be shared.

CONCLUSION

The purpose of the advisory committee is to serve and represent the needs of the local community, and use a strong voice to do so. It is rare to be able to hear firsthand the words of stakeholders and advisory committee members, as they explain the member commitment and their thoughts regarding the process. Hearing the voice of the advisory-committee members allows interested parties to reach a personal and deeper understanding of the reality of how a real-life program works. The advisory committee voices the needs of the entire community, not just those with representation on the committee. The thought-provoking discussions that inspire members to share their ideas and knowledge with the committee to come to a consensus, and the personal experiences of each member, combine to create a more efficiently run program. The committee combines its particular talents and strategies through knowledge-sharing discussions, to generate a plan to implement the project at hand. Using the same critical-thinking skills that students require, the committee focuses on particular training and determines how a project comes to life.

There is no one guideline to structure the perfect committee, and no two committees are just alike. The committee is evolving at each meeting, and the members and the tasks at hand create its structure. The advisory committees have specific agendas and responsibilities that align with their strategic priorities. Some committees are sophisticated and function under a traditional construct; others operate on open construct, and their infrastructure is laid back in nature. One committee structure is no better than the other, as a committee organizes to fit the need for which it was developed, and that of the institution it represents.

REFERENCES

ACT. (2012). Preparing community college students for jobs and careers. Washington, D.C. Retrieved from http://act.rg/research/policymakers/pdf/changing_lives.pdf

ACT. (2016). Job profiling. Washington, D.C. Retrieved from http://www.act.org/content/act/en/products-and-services/workforce-solutions/act-workkeys/job-profiling.html

Allingham, M. (2002). *Choice Theory*. New York, NY: Oxford University Press. doi:10.1093/actrade/9780192803030.001.0001

American Association of Community Colleges. (2013). *Community colleges past to present.* Retrieved from http://www.aacc.nche.edu/AboutCC/history/Pages/pasttopresent.aspx

American Association of Community Colleges and National Center on Education and the Economy. (2009). *Sustaining Partnerships for Regional Economic Growth* (pp. 20–29). Washington, D.C.: American Association of Community Colleges.

Baber, A. (2011). Using community colleges to build a STEM-skilled workforce. *NGA Center for Best Practices.* Retrieved from http://www.nga.org/cms/home/nga-center-for-best-practices/center-publications/page-edu-publications/col2-content/main-content-list/using-community-colleges-to-buil.html

Benigni, V., Ferguson, D., & McGee, B. (2011). Establishing a "renown-gown" relationship: The role of advisory boards in communication programs. Retrieved from http://web.b.ebscohost.com.lib-e2.lib.ttu.edu/ehost/pdfviewer/pdfviewer?sid=8d8ede9c-90be-48fd-9764-5d0d90b803c1%40sessionmgr111&vid=23&hid=123

Bess, J. L., & Dee, J. R. (2008). *Understanding college and university organizations: Theories for effective policy and practice* (Vol. II). City, VA: Stylus.

Beyer, B. K. (1995). Critical thinking and problem-solving. Retrieved from http://www.utc.edu/walker-center-teaching-learning/teaching-resources/ct-ps.php

Bray, J. (2011, January 17). Career and technical colleges can help retrain the unemployed. *The Chronicle of Higher Education.* Retrieved from http://chronicle.com/article/CareerTechnical-Colleges/125977/

Burke, L., & Miller, M. (1999). Taking the mystery out of intuitive decision-making. Retrieved from http://aspnet.cob.ohio.edu/mc/pmba_co_3/Class/CMBA602Strategic/TheMaterialReadings/Module%202%20Readings/R%234%20Taking%20the%20Mystery%20out%20of%20Intuitive%20Decision%20Making.pdf

Carlson, P., Holm, R., & Uvalde, R. (2011). Building regional partnerships for economic growth and opportunity. *Jobs for the Future.* Retrieved from http://futureworks-web.com/pdfs/Building_Regional_Partnerships.pdf

Carson, (2011). A meta-analysis of different forms of shared leadership-team performance relations. Retrieved from http://jom.sagepub.com/content/early/2014/03/06/0149206314525205

Cohen, A., & Brawer, F. (2008). *The American community college.* San Francisco, CA: Jossey-Bass, Inc.

Cohen, A., Brawer, F. B., & Kisker, C. B. (2013). *The American community college.* San Francisco, CA: Jossey-Bass, Inc.

Collin College. (2011). Advisory committee handbook. Retrieved from http://www.cc.edu/handbook/advisory.html

Davis, J. L., & Davis, H. (2009). The learning Organization implemented in education through advisory committees. Retrieved from http://web.b.ebscohost.com.lib-e2.lib.ttu.edu/ehost/pdfviewer/pdfviewer?vid=4&sid=8d8ede9c-90be-48fd-9764-5d0d90b803c1%40sessionmgr111&hid=123

Day, M. (2001). Faculty perceptions of advisory committee effectiveness at two-year technical college. *Journal of Education for Business, 110*(2), 194–198.

DiMattina, C. (n. d.). Lessons in collaboration: Principles in the governance of an industry advisory board. Retrieved from https://www.acteonline.org/uploadedFiles/Assets_and_Documents/Global/files/ Publications/RPB_IndustryAdvisoryBoards.pdf

Dixon, H. (1990). *Communication*. Houston, TX: Washington and Lee University.

Dougherty, K. J., & Townsend, B. K. (2006). Community college missions: A theoretical and historical perspective. New Direction for Community Colleges, (136), 5-13.

GIPWE. (2010, 2015). Guidelines for instructional workforce education. Texas Higher Education Coordinating Board.

Greenstone, M., & Looney, A. (2011). *Building America's job skills with effective workforce programs: A training strategy to raise wages and increase work opportunities*. The Hamilton Project. Retrieved from http://www.brookings.edu/~/media/research/files/papers/2011/11/training%%20 looney/11_training_greenstone_looney.pdf

Hodges, R. (2012). *The road half traveled*. East Lansing, MI: Michigan State University Press.

Jacobs, R. (2007). Emergence of Workforce Development. *Economicmodeling*. Retrieved from www.economicmodeling.com/resources/wp-content/uploads/2007/11/jacobs_hawley-emergenceofworkforcedevelopment.pdf

Johnson, N., Oliff, P., & Williams, E. (2011). An update on state budget cuts. Retrieved from http://www.mobilelottery.com/wp-content/uploads/2010/05/Update-On-State-Budget-Cuts.pdf

Jones, G. (2006). *Organizational theory design and change* (5th ed.). Saddle River, NJ: Prentice Hall.

Kazis, R. (2011). *Brookings-Rockefeller Project on state metropolitan innovation*. Washington, D.C.: Jobs for the Future.

Kerka, S. (2002). *Effective advisory committees*. [ERIC Information Analyses ED463411]. Retrieved from ehis.ebscohost.com.lib-e2.lib.ttu.edu

Kilcrease, K. M. (2011). Faculty perceptions of business advisory boards: The challenge for effective communication. *Journal of Education for Business*, *86*(2), 78–83. doi:10.1080/08832323.2010.480989

Kress, A. M. (2012). A community-based approach to growing the middle-sill workforce. Community College Week. Retrieved from http://www.ccwee.com/news/templates/template.aspx?articleid=3015&zoneid=7

Lane Community College. (2013). CAHM Successful Committee Presentation. Retrieved from http://www.lanecc.edu/ctecc/advisory-committees

Meeder, H. & Pawlowski, B. (2012). Building advisory boards that matter. *Techniques*, *2*(28).

Mintzberg, H. (1979). *The structuring of organizations*. Upper Saddle River, NJ: Prentice Hall.

National Center for Education Statistics. (2010). *Career/Technical Education (CTE) Statistics*. (Table P108). Retrieved from http://nces.ed.gov/surveys/ctes/ tables/P108.asp

National Center for Education Statistics. (2012). *Higher education: Gaps in access and persistence study*. Retrieved from http://nces.ed.gov/pubs2012/2012046/ index.asp

National Center for Education Statistics. (2012). U.S. Background Information Prepared for the OECD Postsecondary Vocational Education and Training "Skills Beyond School" Study. Retrieved from http://nces.ed.gov/surveys/ctes/pdf/Postsec VET.pdf

National Council for Excellence in Critical Thinking. (1987). Defining critical thinking. Retrieved from http://www.criticalthinking.org/pages/defining-critical-thinking/766

Northouse, P. G. (2013). *Leadership: Theory and practice*. Los Angeles, CA: Sage Publishing.

Oliff, P., Palacios, V., Johnson, I., & Leachman, M. (2013). Recent deep state higher education cuts may harm students and the economy for years to come. Retrieved from http://www.cbpp.org/files/3-19-13sfp.pdf

Paul, R. W. (1995). Critical thinking. Retrieved from http://isites.harvard.edu/fs/docs/icb.topic265890.files/Critical_Thinking_File/06_CT_Exten

Perna, L. (2012). *Preparing today's students for tomorrow's jobs in metropolitan America*. Philadelphia, PA: University of Pennsylvania Press.

Price, D. V., & Roberts, B. (2009). Improving student success by strengthening developmental education in community colleges: The role of state policy. The Working Poor Families Project. Retrieved from http://www.workingpoorfamilies.org/pdfs/WPFP_policybrief_winter08-09.pdf

Sena, M., Sena, J. A., & Crable, E. A. (2010). Faculty perceptions on the goals and achievements of information executive board information. Retrieved from http://isedj.org/8/41/ISEDJ.8(41).Sena.pdf

Soares, L. The power of the education-industry partnership. Retrieved from http://american progress.org/issues/labor/report/2010/10/04/8518/thepoweroftheeducation

Spector, B. (2012). *Implementing organizational change: Theory into practice* (3rd ed.). Saddle River, NJ: Prentice Hall.

Tesluk, P. E., & Marrone, J. A. (2011). Shared leadership in teams. Retrieved from http://amj.aom .org/content/50/5/1217.abstract

Texas Higher Education Coordinating Board. (2014). *Advisory Boards.* Retrieved from http://www.thecb.state.tx.us/index.cfm?objectid=8C1EF7E7-A71E-47E6-53FE5EFA82F3880C

Texas Workforce Commission. (2013). Community & Workforce Partners. Retrieved from http://www.twc.state.tx.us/customers/cwp/community-workforce-partners.html

KEY TERMS AND DEFINITIONS

Applied Technology: Career and technical education in schools, institutions, and educational programs, which specializes in skilled trades, applied sciences, modern technologies, and career.

Articulation Agreement: A partnership between colleges and four-year universities, in which students move seamlessly from one institution to another.

Best Practices: A method or technique that has been generally accepted because it produces results that are superior to those achieved by other means or because it has become a standard way of doing things.

Career Technical Education (CTE): Terminology used by some institutions because of the identification associated with job placement, especially in the high-school setting.

Contact Hour: The number of classroom hours the student and professor actually meet.

Critical Thinking: The intellectually disciplined process of actively and skillfully conceptualizing, applying, analyzing, synthesizing, and/or evaluating information gathered from, or generated by, observation, experience, reflection, reasoning, or communication, as a guide to belief and action.

Curriculum: The aggregation of courses of study given in a school, college, or university.

Organizational Approach: Based on the organization's needs, a conceptual construct based on general systems theory.

Oversight Board: Body within the department of education that provides general governance, supervision, and support.

Practitioners: A person engaged in the practice of a profession or occupation.

Programmatic Design: Precise project footprints or specific design.

Reciprocal Relationships: Relationships that require participants to mutually participate and do something similar for each party that is mutually beneficial to both parties.

Stakeholder: Anyone having an interest in a project, such as investors, employees, customers, suppliers, students, administrators, faculty, businesses, industry, and individuals.

Sustainable Economic Development: Measures the country's well-being and how well a country is performing to improve or sustain the dimensions of development, based on data.

Conclusion

The purpose of the advisory committee is to provide judicious guidance within and throughout a vast number of fields spanning across education, business, industry, medical and/or government. In addition, cross collaboration, and input from these fields within an advisory committee can expand and improve cross disciplinary outcomes across fields. The advisory committee offers a platform to share ideas, strategies, recommendations, perspectives, experiences, and expertise that reflects a collective knowledge. The decisions and expertise of key individuals in business and industry that are enlisted to assist on educational advisory committees leads to the creation of a quality workforce. Community involvement is central to the success of committees as well as the input of local citizens. Diverse perspectives are collected and discussed to form cohesive recommendations as a group. The discussion herewith of advisory committees had a narrow conversation and focus on community colleges and biomedical research, since both have increased benefits from diverse advisory committees. This communication details some of the best practices for advisory committees that institutions can implement to develop progressive ways to broaden reach to specific goals.

Even though advisory committees are mandated as part of the community college and increasingly beneficial to implement in biomedical research educational guidelines; other businesses and industries have taken notice of their effectiveness and are implementing this practice. The design of the advisory committee rationalizes the high stakes of decision-making for institutions and organizations based off a group of well-constructed experts in any particular field. The area of education is especially able to utilize advisory committees, due to the heavy constraints placed on budgets as a result of continual budget cuts. Committees serve as a streamlined approach to spending and are used by business and industry as a central component to help advise and assist with difficult decisions. In addition, a new area for workforce development is the use of educational advisory committees that elicit advice, input, and resources from community and industry stakeholders, to improve the education-workforce transition.

In biomedical research education, it is increasingly important to foster collaborative relationships with stakeholders to improve workforce development, leadership, decision-making, and improve outcomes in the current needs of training, workforce development, formative partnerships, and best practices. Biomedical research education is heavily supported by federal and private grants, and both government and the private-industry sector play critical roles in developing partnerships to guide funding grants, project development, management, employment and outreach opportunities. One of the critical problems that biomedical research education faces in many respects, is the specificity of training and often the lack of educational diversity of the programs offered at research institutions. Such programs often lack the development of additional critical skills to improve the transition into other critical employment fields and opportunities that often do not have much to do with biomedical research, and everything to do with a number of additional skills that are inadvertently missed during the period of training. It is in this manuscript that it is observed that advisory committees can act as efficient vehicles to provide educational guidance, carry knowledge to improve curriculum development, assess workforce development, and provide leadership and best decision-making practices. To this end, the model of advisory committees in guiding community college education, workforce development and training, seemed to be an ideal analogy to the development and implementation of advisory committees to the biomedical research field.

Partnerships joined through the advisory committee enables businesses, medical, and educational stakeholders to combine resources, equipment, and knowledge to create a trained supply of skilled workers. Advisory committees are ideally made up of local professionals sharing their knowledge of skills required, updates in regulations, and current trends. The workforce programs are designed to match the needs of business and industry already established in an area. With advances in technology and workforce demands, businesses will need to work closely with educational institutions and others to provide a skilled workforce to keep up with the changing technology that society requires. This partnership with business and industry leads to the development of best practices, including, internships, support for students, accelerated degree completion, tracking of student progress, the designing of new curriculum, shared facilities, and additional resources.

It is important to create a diverse medical research workforce that will be able to improve and advance science while promoting health. The value of biomedical research has been well established in promoting health advancement, public education, outreach, and innovation. Advisory Committees serve well in developing and implementing recommendations within the medical field. Advisory Committees are not foreign in the medical field in providing guidance, leadership, best practices guidance, project development, and developing collaborative opportunities; however, in promoting biomedical research workforce development, an especially good opportunity to implement such committees, can be of great interest to provide workforce leadership guidance during a time when an increase in interest in biomedical research training and a decrease in funding opportunities has resulted in lagging employment opportunities for newly trained scientists. It has not been long since biomedical research graduates have looked at other fields for alternative job opportunities that deviate from the traditional academic path.

As it is often the case in meeting the needs of the industrial and the business-centered sector, advisory committees serve numerous purposes within biomedical research education and training. This ranges from developing a curriculum, assessing present and future needs in the academic research arena, and maintaining a successful record of grant acquisition, to the impact on public health and outreach, advancements in scientific policy, and maintenance of open communication methods, and scientific innovation and entrepreneurship. The implementation of the right advisory committee with the best suited individuals to meet the needs and goals of such advisory committee is increasingly important. An advisory committee has a greater chance of success by including individuals who are proven sound decision-makers. Including experienced and knowledgeable members that are experts in their field on the committee who already have proven decision-making skills and know what questions to ask of the group will lead to accurate decisions. A well-tested and practiced leader's judgement has the ability to justify, learn, and adjust to mistakes by finding solutions and working together with the committee.

At the community college level, advisory committees are instrumental in developing a local and impactful community programs based on the needs of the surrounding businesses and industries. There is a number of issues that may warrant further discussion and attention regarding the appropriateness of advisory committees. Additional issues warranting future discussions and research are the impact of the international community in biomedical research and training assessments that may be warranted as determined by advisory committees. In this work, the appropriateness of advisory committees that elevates the educational and developmental goals in community colleges is directly translated into the biomedical research education arena.

FUTURE RESEARCH

Based on the current research findings regarding advisory committees and their propitious outcomes, it is recommended to consult with organizations that have currently implemented advisory committees that extend outside academic advising, and seek to improve external relations with industry, government and public interest groups to improve workforce development. Institutions are creatively utilizing committees for a variety of outcomes in biomedical research education, ranging from one specific purpose such as thesis advisory committees, to the continual engagement and presence of representative parties within the committee, such as trainee/student-administration-staff groups geared towards improving trainee research experiences. The utilization of an advisory committee for such purposes, seeks to find innovative concepts to research and develop conclusions about best practices with group dynamics, participants, novel areas of concern/interest to yield improvements.

The use of case studies of particularly successful advisory committees can unveil best practices of such committees; additionally, these studies can serve to develop frameworks in building committees that will obtain desired outcomes in a number of different settings. When developing case studies, it is important to reach engagement and understanding of successful advisory committees, the capacity in which these have served, understanding of committee members overall experience, identification of practices that have yielded successful outcomes, understanding of changing dynamics during the development, inception and working process of such committee, and recognition of the strengths that have yielded such a successful committee. In addition, case studies must reflect the modification of the end goals when the advisory committee is met with downturns and obstacles, such as changing committee members, budget cuts, diminishing resources, developing politics, etc. Concentrating on the full effect of advisory committees, and gaining an understanding of the challenges they face while racing to meet the needs during a time of great demand to a complete slow-down, would be of interest to organizations creating or tweaking their committees.

There is little literature and case study publications of advisory committees in biomedical research education to prompt understanding of how these fully work and how institutions can develop a system to reach educational and training goals. Individual institutions develop their internal advisory committees based on their goals, needs, resources, and understanding of their own particular system. However, increasing the dissemination of such literature would provide a resource for institutions seeking to improve the quality of their training, and the workforce development of their trainees. This concept is the basis on how community colleges operate - by providing the resources (training, man-power) based on the current needs of the community.

An immediate need that can be met, is in developing and growing the literature that will deliver, discuss, and disseminate the information on the structure and outcomes of advisory committees in workforce and biomedical research education. Broadening the research to include interviews of members across state lines to gain details and ascertain if states vary how they implement the recommendations by their committee and if the overall function is similar from state to state.

Argentina Ornelas
University of Texas MD Anderson Cancer Center, USA

Julie Neal
Independent Researcher, USA

Related Readings

To continue IGI Global's long-standing tradition of advancing innovation through emerging research, please find below a compiled list of recommended IGI Global book chapters and journal articles in the areas of teaching practices, professional learning, and curriculum integration. These related readings will provide additional information and guidance to further enrich your knowledge and assist you with your own research.

Abdelaziz, H. A. (2014). Creative Design of Interactive eLearning Activities and Materials (IEAM): A Psycho-Pedagogical Model. *International Journal of Technology Diffusion*, *5*(4), 14–34. doi:10.4018/ijtd.2014100102

Abdelmalak, M. M., & Parra, J. L. (2016). Expanding Learning Opportunities for Graduate Students with HyFlex Course Design. *International Journal of Online Pedagogy and Course Design*, *6*(4), 19–37. doi:10.4018/IJOPCD.2016100102

Abera, B. (2014). Applying a Technological Pedagogical Content Knowledge Framework in Ethiopian English Language Teacher Education. In T. Issa, P. Isaias, & P. Kommers (Eds.), Multicultural Awareness and Technology in Higher Education: Global Perspectives (pp. 286–301). Hershey, PA: IGI Global. doi:10.4018/978-1-4666-5876-9.ch014

Adegbenro, J. B., Gumbo, M. T., & Olugbara, O. O. (2015). Exploring Technological Knowledge of Office Data Processing Teachers: Using Factor Analytic Methods. In M. Niess & H. Gillow-Wiles (Eds.), Handbook of Research on Teacher Education in the Digital Age (pp. 548–576). Hershey, PA: IGI Global. doi:10.4018/978-1-4666-8403-4.ch021

Amador, F., Nobre, A., & Barros, D. (2016). Towards a Model of a Didactics of eLearning: An Application to Education for Sustainable Development. In M. Pinheiro & D. Simões (Eds.), Handbook of Research on Engaging Digital Natives in Higher Education Settings (pp. 396–415). Hershey, PA: IGI Global. doi:10.4018/978-1-5225-0039-1.ch019

Amador, J. M., Kimmons, R., Miller, B. G., Desjardins, C. D., & Hall, C. (2015). Preparing Preservice Teachers to Become Self-Reflective of Their Technology Integration Practices. In M. Niess & H. Gillow-Wiles (Eds.), Handbook of Research on Teacher Education in the Digital Age (pp. 81–107). Hershey, PA: IGI Global. doi:10.4018/978-1-4666-8403-4.ch004

Archambault, L. (2014). Teaching Virtually: Strategies and Challenges in the 21st Century Online Classroom. *International Journal of Online Pedagogy and Course Design*, *4*(1), 1–15. doi:10.4018/ijopcd.2014010101

Arinze, B., Sylla, C., & Amobi, O. (2016). Cloud Computing for Teaching and Learning: Design Strategies. In L. Chao (Ed.), Handbook of Research on Cloud-Based STEM Education for Improved Learning Outcomes (pp. 159–171). Hershey, PA: IGI Global. doi:10.4018/978-1-4666-9924-3.ch011

Aşık, A. (2016). Digital Storytelling and Its Tools for Language Teaching: Perceptions and Reflections of Pre-Service Teachers. *International Journal of Computer-Assisted Language Learning and Teaching*, *6*(1), 55–68. doi:10.4018/IJCALLT.2016010104

Attard, C. (2015). Introducing iPads into Primary Mathematics Classrooms: Teachers' Experiences and Pedagogies. In M. Meletiou-Mavrotheris, K. Mavrou, & E. Paparistodemou (Eds.), Integrating Touch-Enabled and Mobile Devices into Contemporary Mathematics Education (pp. 193–213). Hershey, PA: IGI Global. doi:10.4018/978-1-4666-8714-1.ch009

Baert, H. (2015). Technology Tools, Proficiency, and Integration of Physical Education Teacher Educators. In M. Niess & H. Gillow-Wiles (Eds.), Handbook of Research on Teacher Education in the Digital Age (pp. 223–254). Hershey, PA: IGI Global. doi:10.4018/978-1-4666-8403-4.ch009

Banas, J. R., & York, C. S. (2014). The impact of authentic learning exercises on pre-service teachers motivational beliefs towards technology integration. *International Journal of Information and Communication Technology Education*, *10*(3), 60–76. doi:10.4018/ijicte.2014070105

Barakat, M., & Weiss-Randall, D. N. (2016). Through the Eyes of Students and Faculty: A Conceptual Framework for the Development of Online Courses. In V. Wang (Ed.), Handbook of Research on Learning Outcomes and Opportunities in the Digital Age (pp. 557–584). Hershey, PA: IGI Global. doi:10.4018/978-1-4666-9577-1.ch025

Baran, M. L., & Jones, J. E. (2014). Online Learning: Guidelines for Team Effectiveness. In C. Stevenson & J. Bauer (Eds.), Building Online Communities in Higher Education Institutions: Creating Collaborative Experience (pp. 279–292). Hershey, PA: IGI Global. doi:10.4018/978-1-4666-5178-4.ch015

Barbour, M. K., Adelstein, D., & Morrison, J. (2014). The Forgotten Teachers in K-12 Online Learning: Examining the Perceptions of Teachers Who Develop K-12 Online Courses. *International Journal of Online Pedagogy and Course Design*, *4*(3), 18–33. doi:10.4018/ijopcd.2014070102

Boboc, M. (2014). Connecting Communication to Curriculum and Pedagogy in Online Environments. In C. Stevenson & J. Bauer (Eds.), Building Online Communities in Higher Education Institutions: Creating Collaborative Experience (pp. 132–156). Hershey, PA: IGI Global. doi:10.4018/978-1-4666-5178-4.ch007

Borasi, R., Fredericksen, E., & Miller, D. (2017). From 0 to 60: The Case Study of a School of Education's Successful "Online Start-Up". In K. Shelton & K. Pedersen (Eds.), Handbook of Research on Building (pp. 60–83). Hershey, PA: IGI Global. doi:10.4018/978-1-5225-0877-9.ch004

Bowers, J., & Kumar, P. (2015). Students Perceptions of Teaching and Social Presence: A Comparative Analysis of Face-to-Face and Online Learning Environments. *International Journal of Web-Based Learning and Teaching Technologies*, *10*(1), 27–44. doi:10.4018/ijwltt.2015010103

Bozoglan, B., & Demirer, V. (2015). The Association between Internet Addiction and Psychosocial Variables. In J. Bishop (Ed.), *Psychological and Social Implications Surrounding Internet and Gaming Addiction* (pp. 171–185). Hershey, PA: IGI Global. doi:10.4018/978-1-4666-8595-6.ch010

Breen, P. (2014). Philosophies, Traditional Pedagogy, and New Technologies: A Report on a Case Study of EAP Teachers' Integration of Technology into Traditional Practice. In P. Breen (Ed.), Cases on Teacher Identity (pp. 317–341). Hershey, PA: IGI Global. doi:10.4018/978-1-4666-5990-2.ch013

Brockmeier, F. (2017). Service Learning Online: Preparing to Work in Global Societies with E-Service-Learning. In C. Crosby & F. Brockmeier (Eds.), Student Experiences and Educational Outcomes in Community Engagement for the 21st Century (pp. 150–172). Hershey, PA: IGI Global. doi:10.4018/978-1-5225-0874-8.ch007

Brunvand, S. (2016). Facilitating Student Interaction and Collaboration in a MOOC Environment. In R. Mendoza-Gonzalez (Ed.), User-Centered Design Strategies for Massive Open Online Courses (MOOCs) (pp. 1–14). Hershey, PA: IGI Global. doi:10.4018/978-1-4666-9743-0.ch001

Bull, P. H., & Patterson, G. C. (2016). Strategies to Promote Pedagogical Knowledge Interplay with Technology. In J. Keengwe & G. Onchwari (Eds.), Handbook of Research on Active Learning and the Flipped Classroom Model in the Digital Age (pp. 255–271). Hershey, PA: IGI Global. doi:10.4018/978-1-4666-9680-8.ch013

Bush, S. B., Driskell, S. O., Niess, M. L., Pugalee, D., Rakes, C. R., & Ronau, R. N. (2015). The Impact of Digital Technologies in Mathematics Pre-Service Teacher Preparation over Four Decades. In M. Niess & H. Gillow-Wiles (Eds.), Handbook of Research on Teacher Education in the Digital Age (pp. 1–27). Hershey, PA: IGI Global. doi:10.4018/978-1-4666-8403-4.ch001

Byrd-Poller, L., Farmer, J. L., & Ford, V. (2017). The Role of Leaders in Facilitating Healing After Organizational Trauma. In S. Háša & R. Brunet-Thornton (Eds.), *Impact of Organizational Trauma on Workplace Behavior and Performance* (pp. 318–340). Hershey, PA: IGI Global. doi:10.4018/978-1-5225-2021-4.ch014

Cacho-Elizondo, S., Shahidi, N., & Tossan, V. (2015). Giving Up Smoking Using SMS Messages on your Mobile Phone. In A. Mesquita & C. Tsai (Eds.), *Human Behavior, Psychology, and Social Interaction in the Digital Era* (pp. 72–94). Hershey, PA: IGI Global. doi:10.4018/978-1-4666-8450-8.ch004

Card, S., & Wang, H. (2015). Taking Care to Play: Meaningful Communication in Dementia Care in Chinese Culture. In C. Dick-Muehlke, R. Li, & M. Orleans (Eds.), *Psychosocial Studies of the Individual's Changing Perspectives in Alzheimer's Disease* (pp. 76–103). Hershey, PA: IGI Global. doi:10.4018/978-1-4666-8478-2.ch004

Carrasco, G., & Kinnamon, E. (2017). An Examination of Selfish and Selfless Motives: A Review of the Social Psychological and Behavioral Economics Literature. In R. Ianole (Ed.), *Applied Behavioral Economics Research and Trends* (pp. 93–109). Hershey, PA: IGI Global. doi:10.4018/978-1-5225-1826-6.ch006

Cejka, P., & Mohelska, H. (2017). National Culture Influence on Organisational Trauma: A Conceptual Framework Review. In S. Háša & R. Brunet-Thornton (Eds.), *Impact of Organizational Trauma on Workplace Behavior and Performance* (pp. 162–186). Hershey, PA: IGI Global. doi:10.4018/978-1-5225-2021-4.ch007

Chen, C. (2016). Effective Learning Strategies for the 21st Century: Implications for the E-Learning. In M. Anderson & C. Gavan (Eds.), Developing Effective Educational Experiences through Learning Analytics (pp. 143–169). Hershey, PA: IGI Global. doi:10.4018/978-1-4666-9983-0.ch006

Chen, C., Chiu, P., & Huang, Y. (2015). The Learning Style-Based Adaptive Learning System Architecture. *International Journal of Online Pedagogy and Course Design*, *5*(2), 1–10. doi:10.4018/IJOPCD.2015040101

Chen, R., Lin, T., & Xie, T. (2015). Towards Intelligent Window Layout Management: The Role of Mental Map. In A. Mesquita & C. Tsai (Eds.), *Human Behavior, Psychology, and Social Interaction in the Digital Era* (pp. 146–161). Hershey, PA: IGI Global. doi:10.4018/978-1-4666-8450-8.ch007

Cheng, H. (2017). A TL-TPACK Model on CSL Pre-Service Teachers' Competencies of Online Instruction. In C. Lin, D. Zhang, & B. Zheng (Eds.), Preparing Foreign Language Teachers for Next-Generation Education (pp. 198–225). Hershey, PA: IGI Global. doi:10.4018/978-1-5225-0483-2.ch011

Chuang, S., Lin, S., Chang, T., & Kaewmeesri, R. (2017). Behavioral Intention of Using Social Networking Site: A Comparative Study of Taiwanese and Thai Facebook Users. *International Journal of Technology and Human Interaction*, *13*(1), 61–81. doi:10.4018/IJTHI.2017010104

Cialdella, V. T., Lobato, E. J., & Jordan, J. S. (2017). Wild Architecture: Explaining Cognition via Self-Sustaining Systems. In J. Vallverdú, M. Mazzara, M. Talanov, S. Distefano, & R. Lowe (Eds.), Advanced Research on Biologically Inspired Cognitive Architectures (pp. 41–62). Hershey, PA: IGI Global. doi:10.4018/978-1-5225-1947-8.ch003

Çınar, M., & Tüzün, H. (2016). Web-Based Course Design Models. In M. Pinheiro & D. Simões (Eds.), Handbook of Research on Engaging Digital Natives in Higher Education Settings (pp. 374–395). Hershey, PA: IGI Global. doi:10.4018/978-1-5225-0039-1.ch018

Cleve, R. A., Işık, İ., & Pecanha, V. D. (2017). Sexual Identities in the Workplace: Avoiding Organizational Trauma When Disclosure Occurs – Current Perspectives. In S. Háša & R. Brunet-Thornton (Eds.), *Impact of Organizational Trauma on Workplace Behavior and Performance* (pp. 188–220). Hershey, PA: IGI Global. doi:10.4018/978-1-5225-2021-4.ch008

Conrad, S. S., & Dabbagh, N. (2015). Examining the Factors that Influence how Instructors Provide Feedback in Online Learning Environments. *International Journal of Online Pedagogy and Course Design*, *5*(4), 47–66. doi:10.4018/IJOPCD.2015100104

Contier, A. T., & Torres, L. (2017). Neuroaesthetics: Insights into the Aesthetic Experience of Visual Art. In R. Zuanon (Ed.), *Projective Processes and Neuroscience in Art and Design* (pp. 87–102). Hershey, PA: IGI Global. doi:10.4018/978-1-5225-0510-5.ch006

Courey, S., LePage, P., Blackorby, J., Siker, J., & Nguyen, T. (2015). The Effects of Using Dynabook to Prepare Special Education Teachers to Teach Proportional Reasoning. *International Journal of Web-Based Learning and Teaching Technologies*, *10*(1), 45–64. doi:10.4018/ijwltt.2015010104

Cranton, P., & Thompson, P. (2014). Creating Collaboration in Global Online Learning: Case Studies. In V. Wang (Ed.), Handbook of Research on Education and Technology in a Changing Society (pp. 92–103). Hershey, PA: IGI Global. doi:10.4018/978-1-4666-6046-5.ch007

Crawford, C. M., & Smith, M. S. (2015). Rethinking Bloom's Taxonomy: Implicit Cognitive Vulnerability as an Impetus towards Higher Order Thinking Skills. In Z. Jin (Ed.), *Exploring Implicit Cognition: Learning, Memory, and Social Cognitive Processes* (pp. 86–103). Hershey, PA: IGI Global. doi:10.4018/978-1-4666-6599-6.ch004

de Groot, C., Fogleman, J., & Kern, D. (2015). Using Mobile Technologies to Co-Construct TPACK in Teacher Education. In J. Keengwe & M. Maxfield (Eds.), Advancing Higher Education with Mobile Learning Technologies: Cases (pp. 195–219). Hershey, PA: IGI Global. doi:10.4018/978-1-4666-6284-1.ch011 de Soir, E., & Kleber, R. (2017). Understanding the Core of Psychological Trauma: Trauma in Contemporary French Theory. In S. Háša & R. Brunet-Thornton (Eds.), *Impact of Organizational Trauma on Workplace Behavior and Performance* (pp. 57–75). Hershey, PA: IGI Global. doi:10.4018/978-1-5225-2021-4.ch003

Delgado, J. J. (2017). How Is the Personality of Facebook Customers?: Cloninger's Psychobiological Model of Temperament as a Predictor of SNSs. In M. Dos Santos (Ed.), *Applying Neuroscience to Business Practice* (pp. 191–229). Hershey, PA: IGI Global. doi:10.4018/978-1-5225-1028-4.ch009

Dentale, F., Vecchione, M., & Barbaranelli, C. (2015). Applying the IAT to Assess Big Five Personality Traits: A Brief Review of Measurement and Validity Issues. In Z. Jin (Ed.), *Exploring Implicit Cognition: Learning, Memory, and Social Cognitive Processes* (pp. 1–15). Hershey, PA: IGI Global. doi:10.4018/978-1-4666-6599-6.ch001

Deyoe, M. M., Newman, D. L., & Asaro-Saddler, K. (2014). Moving from Professional Development to Real-Time Use: How are we Changing Students? In J. Keengwe, G. Onchwari, & D. Hucks (Eds.), Literacy Enrichment and Technology Integration in Pre-Service Teacher Education (pp. 160–182). Hershey, PA: IGI Global. doi:10.4018/978-1-4666-4924-8.ch010

Dick, T. P., & Burrill, G. F. (2016). Design and Implementation Principles for Dynamic Interactive Mathematics Technologies. In M. Niess, S. Driskell, & K. Hollebrands (Eds.), Handbook of Research on Transforming Mathematics Teacher Education in the Digital Age (pp. 23–51). Hershey, PA: IGI Global. doi:10.4018/978-1-5225-0120-6.ch002

Díez, J. C., & Saiz-Alvarez, J. M. (2016). Leadership in Social Entrepreneurship: Is It Ability or Skill? In J. Saiz-Álvarez (Ed.), *Handbook of Research on Social Entrepreneurship and Solidarity Economics* (pp. 134–153). Hershey, PA: IGI Global. doi:10.4018/978-1-5225-0097-1.ch008

Dikici, A. (2017). Revisiting the Relationships between Turkish Prospective Teachers' Thinking Styles and Behaviors Fostering Creativity. In N. Silton (Ed.), Exploring the Benefits of Creativity in Education, Media, and the Arts (pp. 136–157). Hershey, PA: IGI Global. doi:10.4018/978-1-5225-0504-4.ch007

Dodd, B. J., Baukal, C. E. Jr, & Ausburn, L. J. (2016). A Post-Positivist Framework for Using and Building Theory in Online Instructional Design. *International Journal of Online Pedagogy and Course Design*, *6*(4), 53–70. doi:10.4018/IJOPCD.2016100104

Driskell, S. O., Bush, S. B., Ronau, R. N., Niess, M. L., Rakes, C. R., & Pugalee, D. K. (2016). Mathematics Education Technology Professional Development: Changes over Several Decades. In M. Niess, S. Driskell, & K. Hollebrands (Eds.), Handbook of Research on Transforming Mathematics Teacher Education in the Digital Age (pp. 107–136). Hershey, PA: IGI Global. doi:10.4018/978-1-5225-0120-6.ch005

Dunston, Y. L., Patterson, G. C., & Bull, P. H. (2016). Faculty Perspectives of Technology-Enhanced Course Redesign. In J. Keengwe & G. Onchwari (Eds.), Handbook of Research on Active Learning and the Flipped Classroom Model in the Digital Age (pp. 150–176). Hershey, PA: IGI Global. doi:10.4018/978-1-4666-9680-8.ch008

Duvall, M., Matranga, A., Foster, A., & Silverman, J. (2016). Mobile Learning: Technology as Mediator of Personal and School Experiences. *International Journal of Game-Based Learning*, *6*(1), 30–42. doi:10.4018/IJGBL.2016010103

Eapen, V., & Walter, A. (2016). Mind the Gap: Developmental Vulnerability and Mental Health. In R. Gopalan (Ed.), Handbook of Research on Diagnosing, Treating, and Managing Intellectual Disabilities (pp. 11–32). Hershey, PA: IGI Global. doi:10.4018/978-1-5225-0089-6.ch002

Edson, A. J., & Thomas, A. (2016). Transforming Preservice Mathematics Teacher Knowledge for and with the Enacted Curriculum: The Case of Digital Instructional Materials. In M. Niess, S. Driskell, & K. Hollebrands (Eds.), Handbook of Research on Transforming Mathematics Teacher Education in the Digital Age (pp. 215–240). Hershey, PA: IGI Global. doi:10.4018/978-1-5225-0120-6.ch009

Fallon, F. (2017). Integrated Information Theory (IIT) and Artificial Consciousness. In J. Vallverdú, M. Mazzara, M. Talanov, S. Distefano, & R. Lowe (Eds.), *Advanced Research on Biologically Inspired Cognitive Architectures* (pp. 1–23). Hershey, PA: IGI Global. doi:10.4018/978-1-5225-1947-8.ch001

Fang, L., & Ha, L. (2015). Do College Students Benefit from Their Social Media Experience?: Social Media Involvement and Its Impact on College Students' Self-Efficacy Perception. In A. Mesquita & C. Tsai (Eds.), *Human Behavior, Psychology, and Social Interaction in the Digital Era* (pp. 259–278). Hershey, PA: IGI Global. doi:10.4018/978-1-4666-8450-8.ch013

Farmer, L. (2014). Technology Impact on New Adult Behavior about Health Information. In V. Wang (Ed.), Handbook of Research on Adult and Community Health Education: Tools, Trends, and Methodologies (pp. 68–81). Hershey, PA: IGI Global. doi:10.4018/978-1-4666-6260-5.ch005

Fasko, D. (2017). Creativity in the Schools: Educational Changes Lately? In N. Silton (Ed.), *Exploring the Benefits of Creativity in Education, Media, and the Arts* (pp. 92–116). Hershey, PA: IGI Global. doi:10.4018/978-1-5225-0504-4.ch005

Fasso, W., Knight, C., & Knight, B. A. (2014). A Learner-Centered Design Framework for E-Learning. *International Journal of Online Pedagogy and Course Design, 4*(4), 44–59. doi:10.4018/ijopcd.2014100104

Fazio, S., & Mitchell, D. B. (2015). Self-Preservation in Individuals with Alzheimer's Disease: Empirical Evidence and the Role of the Social Environment. In C. Dick-Muehlke, R. Li, & M. Orleans (Eds.), *Psychosocial Studies of the Individual's Changing Perspectives in Alzheimer's Disease* (pp. 183–207). Hershey, PA: IGI Global. doi:10.4018/978-1-4666-8478-2.ch008

Feitosa-Santana, C. (2017). Understanding How the Mind Works: The Neuroscience of Perception, Behavior, and Creativity. In R. Zuanon (Ed.), *Projective Processes and Neuroscience in Art and Design* (pp. 239–252). Hershey, PA: IGI Global. doi:10.4018/978-1-5225-0510-5.ch014

Felger, J., & Shafer, K. G. (2016). An Algebra Teacher's Instructional Decision-Making Process with GeoGebra: Thinking with a TPACK Mindset. In M. Niess, S. Driskell, & K. Hollebrands (Eds.), Handbook of Research on Transforming Mathematics Teacher Education in the Digital Age (pp. 493–518). Hershey, PA: IGI Global. doi:10.4018/978-1-5225-0120-6.ch019

Ferris, A. (2017). Creativity in the Emerging Adult. In N. Silton (Ed.), *Exploring the Benefits of Creativity in Education, Media, and the Arts* (pp. 26–49). Hershey, PA: IGI Global. doi:10.4018/978-1-5225-0504-4.ch002

Fife, E., Nelson, C. L., & Clarke, T. B. (2014). Online technological media in the higher education classroom: an exploratory investigation of varied levels of Twitter use. *International Journal of Online Pedagogy and Course Design*, *4*(2), 35–45. doi:10.4018/ijopcd.2014040103

Figg, C., & Jaipal-Jamani, K. (2015). Developing Teacher Knowledge about Gamification as an Instructional Strategy. In M. Niess & H. Gillow-Wiles (Eds.), Handbook of Research on Teacher Education in the Digital Age (pp. 663–690). Hershey, PA: IGI Global. doi:10.4018/978-1-4666-8403-4.ch025

Finger, G. (2015). Improving Initial Teacher Education in Australia: Solutions and Recommendations from the Teaching Teachers for the Future Project. In N. Ololube, P. Kpolovie, & L. Makewa (Eds.), Handbook of Research on Enhancing Teacher Education with Advanced Instructional Technologies (pp. 187–207). Hershey, PA: IGI Global. doi:10.4018/978-1-4666-8162-0.ch010

Flores, A., Park, J., & Bernhardt, S. A. (2016). Learning Mathematics and Technology through Inquiry, Cooperation, and Communication: A Learning Trajectory for Future Mathematics Teachers. In M. Niess, S. Driskell, & K. Hollebrands (Eds.), Handbook of Research on Transforming Mathematics Teacher Education in the Digital Age (pp. 324–352). Hershey, PA: IGI Global. doi:10.4018/978-1-5225-0120-6.ch013

Fogliano, F., & Oliveira, H. C. (2017). Neuroesthetics: Perspectives and Reflections. In R. Zuanon (Ed.), *Projective Processes and Neuroscience in Art and Design* (pp. 52–70). Hershey, PA: IGI Global. doi:10.4018/978-1-5225-0510-5.ch004

Fokides, E. (2016). Pre-Service Teachers, Computers, and ICT Courses: A Troubled Relationship. *International Journal of Information and Communication Technology Education*, *12*(4), 25–36. doi:10.4018/IJICTE.2016100103

Folk, J. R., & Eskenazi, M. A. (2017). Eye Movement Behavior and Individual Differences in Word Identification During Reading. In C. Was, F. Sansosti, & B. Morris (Eds.), *Eye-Tracking Technology Applications in Educational Research* (pp. 66–87). Hershey, PA: IGI Global. doi:10.4018/978-1-5225-1005-5.ch004

Foster, A., & Shah, M. (2016). Knew Me and New Me: Facilitating Student Identity Exploration and Learning through Game Integration. *International Journal of Gaming and Computer-Mediated Simulations, 8*(3), 39–58. doi:10.4018/IJGCMS.2016070103

Franco, M., Ortiz, T. V., Amorim, H. A., & Faber, J. (2017). Can We Induce a Cognitive Representation of a Prosthetic Arm by Means of Crossmodal Stimuli? In R. Zuanon (Ed.), *Projective Processes and Neuroscience in Art and Design* (pp. 182–204). Hershey, PA: IGI Global. doi:10.4018/978-1-5225-0510-5.ch011

Frazier, L. C., & Palmer, B. M. (2015). Effective Online Learning Begins with Effective Teacher Preparation. In T. Heafner, R. Hartshorne, & T. Petty (Eds.), Exploring the Effectiveness of Online Education in K-12 Environments (pp. 148–168). Hershey, PA: IGI Global. doi:10.4018/978-1-4666-6383-1.ch008

G., L. (2017). Psychosocial Intervention Studies for Street Children with Substance Abuse. In B. Prasad (Ed.), *Chronic Mental Illness and the Changing Scope of Intervention Strategies, Diagnosis, and Treatment* (pp. 237-257). Hershey, PA: IGI Global. doi:10.4018/978-1-5225-0519-8.ch013

Gallagher-Lepak, S., & Vandenhouten, C. (2016). E-Learning and Faculty Development in Higher Education: A Comprehensive Project. In B. Khan (Ed.), Revolutionizing Modern Education through Meaningful E-Learning Implementation (pp. 226–244). Hershey, PA: IGI Global. doi:10.4018/978-1-5225-0466-5.ch012

Gallego, J. (2017). Organizational Trauma and Change Management. In S. Háša & R. Brunet-Thornton (Eds.), Impact of Organizational Trauma on Workplace Behavior and Performance (pp. 140–161). Hershey, PA: IGI Global. doi:10.4018/978-1-5225-2021-4.ch006

Galvin, J. E., & Kelleher, M. E. (2015). Dementia and Other Neurocognitive Disorders: An Overview. In C. Dick-Muehlke, R. Li, & M. Orleans (Eds.), *Psychosocial Studies of the Individual's Changing Perspectives in Alzheimer's Disease* (pp. 104–130). Hershey, PA: IGI Global. doi:10.4018/978-1-4666-8478-2.ch005

Gardner, M. K., & Strayer, D. L. (2017). What Cognitive Psychology Can Tell Us About Educational Computer Games. In R. Zheng & M. Gardner (Eds.), Handbook of Research on Serious Games for Educational Applications (pp. 1–18). Hershey, PA: IGI Global. doi:10.4018/978-1-5225-0513-6.ch001

Garg, B., Khanna, P., & Khanna, A. (2017). Chronic Mental Illness and the Changing Scope of Intervention Strategies, Diagnosis, and Treatment in Child and Adolescent Population. In B. Prasad (Ed.), *Chronic Mental Illness and the Changing Scope of Intervention Strategies, Diagnosis, and Treatment* (pp. 258–269). Hershey, PA: IGI Global. doi:10.4018/978-1-5225-0519-8.ch014

Gautreau, C. S., Stang, K. K., Street, C., & Guillaume, A. (2014). Making the Move: Supporting Faculty in the Transition to Blended or Online Courses. *International Journal of Online Pedagogy and Course Design*, *4*(1), 27–42. doi:10.4018/ijopcd.2014010103

Giannouli, V. (2017). Creativity and Giftedness: A Study of Attitudes. In N. Silton (Ed.), *Exploring the Benefits of Creativity in Education, Media, and the Arts* (pp. 179–197). Hershey, PA: IGI Global. doi:10.4018/978-1-5225-0504-4.ch009

Gikandi, J. W. (2015). Towards a Theory of Formative Assessment in Online Higher Education. In J. Keengwe (Ed.), Handbook of Research on Educational Technology Integration and Active Learning (pp. 292–316). Hershey, PA: IGI Global. doi:10.4018/978-1-4666-8363-1.ch014

Gikandi, J. W. (2017). Computer-Supported Collaborative Learning and Assessment: A Strategy for Developing Online Learning Communities in Continuing Education. In J. Keengwe & G. Onchwari (Eds.), Handbook of Research on Learner-Centered Pedagogy in Teacher Education and Professional Development (pp. 309–333). Hershey, PA: IGI Global. doi:10.4018/978-1-5225-0892-2.ch017

Gillow-Wiles, H., & Niess, M. L. (2015). Engaging Google Docs to Support Collaboration and Reflection in Online Teacher Education. In M. Niess & H. Gillow-Wiles (Eds.), Handbook of Research on Teacher Education in the Digital Age (pp. 635–662). Hershey, PA: IGI Global. doi:10.4018/978-1-4666-8403-4.ch024

Gillow-Wiles, H., & Niess, M. L. (2016). A Reconstructed Conception of Learner Engagement in Technology Rich Online Learning Environments. In M. Niess, S. Driskell, & K. Hollebrands (Eds.), Handbook of Research on Transforming Mathematics Teacher Education in the Digital Age (pp. 577–607). Hershey, PA: IGI Global. doi:10.4018/978-1-5225-0120-6.ch022

Golden, J. E., & Brown, V. (2017). A Holistic Professional Development Model: A Case Study to Support Faculty Transition to Online Teaching. In C. Martin & D. Polly (Eds.), Handbook of Research on Teacher Education and Professional Development (pp. 259–284). Hershey, PA: IGI Global. doi:10.4018/978-1-5225-1067-3.ch014

Goodson-Espy, T., & Poling, L. (2015). Interactive Whiteboards: Preparing Secondary Mathematics Teachers to Avoid Catch-22. In D. Polly (Ed.), Cases on Technology Integration in Mathematics Education (pp. 288–307). Hershey, PA: IGI Global. doi:10.4018/978-1-4666-6497-5.ch014

Gopalan, R. T. (2016). Intellectual Disability: From History to Recent Trends. In R. Gopalan (Ed.), *Handbook of Research on Diagnosing, Treating, and Managing Intellectual Disabilities* (pp. 1–10). Hershey, PA: IGI Global. doi:10.4018/978-1-5225-0089-6.ch001

Guan, S. (2014). Internet-Based Technology Use in Second Language Learning: A Systematic Review. *International Journal of Cyber Behavior, Psychology and Learning*, *4*(4), 69–81. doi:10.4018/ijcbpl.2014100106

Gupta, S., Taneja, S., & Kumar, N. (2015). Redefining the Classroom: Integration of Open and Classroom Learning in Higher Education. In E. McKay & J. Lenarcic (Eds.), Macro-Level Learning through Massive Open Online Courses (MOOCs) (pp. 168–182). Hershey, PA: IGI Global. doi:10.4018/978-1-4666-8324-2.ch010

Hacker, D. J. (2017). The Role of Metacognition in Learning via Serious Games. In R. Zheng & M. Gardner (Eds.), *Handbook of Research on Serious Games for Educational Applications* (pp. 19–40). Hershey, PA: IGI Global. doi:10.4018/978-1-5225-0513-6.ch002

Hadjileontiadou, S. J., Dias, S. B., Diniz, J. A., & Hadjileontiadis, L. J. (2015). Understanding Online Learning Environments (OLEs). In Fuzzy Logic-Based Modeling in Collaborative and Blended Learning (pp. 18-50). Hershey, PA: IGI Global. doi:10.4018/978-1-4666-8705-9.ch002

Halder, S., & Mahato, A. (2017). Cognitive Remediation Therapy in Chronic Schizophrenia. In B. Prasad (Ed.), *Chronic Mental Illness and the Changing Scope of Intervention Strategies, Diagnosis, and Treatment* (pp. 292–307). Hershey, PA: IGI Global. doi:10.4018/978-1-5225-0519-8.ch016

Harkness, S. J. (2014). Program Administration and Implementation of an Online Learning Initiative at a Historically Black College University. In M. Orleans (Ed.), Cases on Critical and Qualitative Perspectives in Online Higher Education (pp. 44–60). Hershey, PA: IGI Global. doi:10.4018/978-1-4666-5051-0.ch003

Harrington, R. A., Driskell, S. O., Johnston, C. J., Browning, C. A., & Niess, M. L. (2016). Technological Pedagogical Content Knowledge: Preparation and Support of Mathematics Teachers. In M. Niess, S. Driskell, & K. Hollebrands (Eds.), Handbook of Research on Transforming Mathematics Teacher Education in the Digital Age (pp. 1–22). Hershey, PA: IGI Global. doi:10.4018/978-1-5225-0120-6.ch001

Heins, S., Heins, G., & Dick-Muehlke, C. (2015). Steve's Story: Living with Mild Cognitive Impairment. In C. Dick-Muehlke, R. Li, & M. Orleans (Eds.), *Psychosocial Studies of the Individual's Changing Perspectives in Alzheimer's Disease* (pp. 33–60). Hershey, PA: IGI Global. doi:10.4018/978-1-4666-8478-2.ch002

Ndinguri, E., Machtmes, K., Machtmes, R. J., & Hill, J. (2015). Exploring How Women Entrepreneurs Use Technology for Idea Generation. *International Journal of E-Entrepreneurship and Innovation*, *5*(2), 24–38. doi:10.4018/IJEEI.2015070102

Nguyen, C., Davis, H., Sharrock, G., & Hempsall, K. (2014). Realising the Potential of MOOCs in Developing Capacity for Tertiary Education Managers. *Information Resources Management Journal*, *27*(2), 47–60. doi:10.4018/irmj.2014040104

Nthomang, K. (2016). Inspiring Poor Women to Empower Themselves: Insights and Lessons from Botswana. *International Journal of Civic Engagement and Social Change*, *3*(2), 39–53. doi:10.4018/IJCESC.2016040103

Nwosu, M., Igwe, K., & Emezie, N. (2014). Women Artisans Information Needs, Sources and Seeking Behaviour and the Implication for Empowerment in a Semi-Urban Area in Nigeria. *International Journal of Civic Engagement and Social Change*, *1*(4), 47–63. doi:10.4018/IJCESC.2014100103

Ojokoh, B. A., Adeola, O. S., Isinkaye, F. O., & Abraham, C. (2014). Career Choices in Information and Communication Technology among South Western Nigerian Women. *Journal of Global Information Management*, *22*(2), 48–77. doi:10.4018/jgim.2014040104

Ololube, N. P., Agbor, C. N., & Agabi, C. O. (2017). Effective Leadership and Management in Universities through Quality Management Models. In N. Baporikar (Ed.), *Innovation and Shifting Perspectives in Management Education* (pp. 224–245). Hershey, PA: IGI Global. doi:10.4018/978-1-5225-1019-2.ch010

Özbaş, M. (2016). Chaotic and Complex Situations in Girls' Education: Problems and Solutions. In Ş. Erçetin (Ed.), *Applied Chaos and Complexity Theory in Education* (pp. 1–10). Hershey, PA: IGI Global. doi:10.4018/978-1-5225-0460-3.ch001

Ozdemir, E. A., & Dikilitaş, K. (2016). Teachers' Professional Development in the Digitized World: A Sample Blended Learning Environment for Educational Technology Training. In K. Dikilitaş (Ed.), *Innovative Professional Development Methods and Strategies for STEM Education* (pp. 115–125). Hershey, PA: IGI Global. doi:10.4018/978-1-4666-9471-2.ch007

Palmeira, M. (2014). Frontline Employees' Self-Perception of Ageism, Sexism, and Lookism: Comparative Analyses of Prejudice and Discrimination in Fashion and Food Retailing. In F. Musso & E. Druica (Eds.), *Handbook of Research on Retailer-Consumer Relationship Development* (pp. 275–296). Hershey, PA: IGI Global. doi:10.4018/978-1-4666-6074-8.ch015

Parsa, F. (2016). Challenges of Iranian Women to Change the Gender Discriminatory Law. In N. Mahtab, S. Parker, F. Kabir, T. Haque, A. Sabur, & A. Sowad (Eds.), Discourse Analysis as a Tool for Understanding Gender Identity, Representation, and Equality (pp. 74–89). Hershey, PA: IGI Global. doi:10.4018/978-1-5225-0225-8.ch004

Patiño, B. E. (2017). New Generation Management by Convergence and Individual Identity: A Systemic and Human-Oriented Approach. In N. Baporikar (Ed.), Innovation and Shifting Perspectives in Management Education (pp. 119–143). Hershey, PA: IGI Global. doi:10.4018/978-1-5225-1019-2.ch006

Pereira, C. E. (2014). Emerging Digital Technologies and Women's Leadership in Global Business. In P. Smith & T. Cockburn (Eds.), Impact of Emerging Digital Technologies on Leadership in Global Business (pp. 255–279). Hershey, PA: IGI Global. doi:10.4018/978-1-4666-6134-9.ch014

Phiri, S. (2016). Political Dis-Empowerment of Women by ICTs: The Case of the Zambian Elections. In J. Wilson & N. Gapsiso (Eds.), Overcoming Gender Inequalities through Technology Integration (pp. 54–67). Hershey, PA: IGI Global. doi:10.4018/978-1-4666-9773-7.ch003

Pimpa, N., & Hooi, E. (2014). Modern Leadership in Singaporean and Thai Organizational Contexts. *International Journal of Knowledge-Based Organizations*, *4*(4), 21–35. doi:10.4018/ijkbo.2014100102

Prescott, J., & Bogg, J. (2014). Issues Career Women Face. In Gender Divide and the Computer Game Industry (pp. 170–192). Hershey, PA: IGI Global. doi:10.4018/978-1-4666-4534-9.ch008

Rathore, A. K., Tuli, N., & Ilavarasan, P. V. (2016). Pro-Business or Common Citizen?: An Analysis of an Indian Woman CEOs Tweets. *International Journal of Virtual Communities and Social Networking*, *8*(1), 19–29. doi:10.4018/IJVCSN.2016010102

Renna, P., Izzo, C., & Romaniello, T. (2016). The Business Process Management Systems to Support Continuous Improvements. In W. Nuninger & J. Châtelet (Eds.), Handbook of Research on Quality Assurance and Value Management in Higher Education (pp. 237–256). Hershey, PA: IGI Global. doi:10.4018/978-1-5225-0024-7.ch009

Ro, H. K., & McIntosh, K. (2016). Constructing Conducive Environment for Women of Color in Engineering Undergraduate Education. In U. Thomas & J. Drake (Eds.), Critical Research on Sexism and Racism in STEM Fields (pp. 23–48). Hershey, PA: IGI Global. doi:10.4018/978-1-5225-0174-9.ch002

Robby, M. A. (2014). Faculty and Chair Perceptions and Ratings about System-Wide Assessments in the Higher Colleges of Technology. In V. Wang (Ed.), Advanced Research in Adult Learning and Professional Development: Tools, Trends, and Methodologies (pp. 102–120). Hershey, PA: IGI Global. doi:10.4018/978-1-4666-4615-5.ch004

Roberts, C. (2017). Advancing Women Leaders in Academe: Creating a Culture of Inclusion. In S. Mukerji & P. Tripathi (Eds.), Handbook of Research on Administration, Policy, and Leadership in Higher Education (pp. 256–273). Hershey, PA: IGI Global. doi:10.4018/978-1-5225-0672-0.ch012

Runté, M., & Runté, R. (2017). The Evolving Discourse of the Purpose of Higher Education: The Rhetoric of Higher Education Reform. In S. Mukerji & P. Tripathi (Eds.), Handbook of Research on Administration, Policy, and Leadership in Higher Education (pp. 532–548). Hershey, PA: IGI Global. doi:10.4018/978-1-5225-0672-0.ch021

Samya, A. S. (2016). Diversity or Dilemma: The Cry for Social Freedom of MSM People Living in Dhaka City. In N. Mahtab, S. Parker, F. Kabir, T. Haque, A. Sabur, & A. Sowad (Eds.), Revealing Gender Inequalities and Perceptions in South Asian Countries through Discourse Analysis (pp. 1–19). Hershey, PA: IGI Global. doi:10.4018/978-1-5225-0279-1.ch001

Sanders, S. L., & Orbe, M. P. (2016). TIPs to Maximize Meaningful Professional Development Programs and Initiatives: A Case Study in Theoretically-Grounded Diversity Education. In C. Scott & J. Sims (Eds.), Developing Workforce Diversity Programs, Curriculum, and Degrees in Higher Education (pp. 235–257). Hershey, PA: IGI Global. doi:10.4018/978-1-5225-0209-8.ch013

Scott, C. L. (2016). The Diverse Voices Conference: Expanding Diversity Education Beyond the Classroom. In C. Scott, & J. Sims (Eds.), *Developing Workforce Diversity Programs, Curriculum, and Degrees in Higher Education*(pp. 62-73). Hershey, PA: IGI Global. doi:10.4018/978-1-5225-0209-8.ch004

Shambaugh, N. (2017). Ongoing and Systematic Academic Program Review. In S. Mukerji & P. Tripathi (Eds.), Handbook of Research on Administration, Policy, and Leadership in Higher Education (pp. 141–156). Hershey, PA: IGI Global. doi:10.4018/978-1-5225-0672-0.ch007

Shumilova, Y., & Cai, Y. (2016). Three Approaches to Competing for Global Talent: Role of Higher Education. In K. Bista & C. Foster (Eds.), Global Perspectives and Local Challenges Surrounding International Student Mobility (pp. 114–135). Hershey, PA: IGI Global. doi:10.4018/978-1-4666-9746-1.ch007

Sims, C. H. (2015). Genderized Workplace Lookism in the U.S. and Abroad: Implications for Organization and Career Development Professionals. In C. Hughes (Ed.), Impact of Diversity on Organization and Career Development (pp. 105–127). Hershey, PA: IGI Global. doi:10.4018/978-1-4666-7324-3.ch005

Smith, A. R. (2017). Ensuring Quality: The Faculty Role in Online Higher Education. In K. Shelton & K. Pedersen (Eds.), Handbook of Research on Building, Growing, and Sustaining Quality E-Learning Programs (pp. 210–231). Hershey, PA: IGI Global. doi:10.4018/978-1-5225-0877-9.ch011

Smith, C. R. (2015). Black, Female, and Foreign: The Triple-Invisibility of Afro-Caribbean Women in the Academy. In M. Zhou (Ed.), Supporting Multiculturalism and Gender Diversity in University Settings (pp. 74–100). Hershey, PA: IGI Global. doi:10.4018/978-1-4666-8321-1.ch005

Smyth, R., Bossu, C., & Stagg, A. (2016). Toward an Open Empowered Learning Model of Pedagogy in Higher Education. In S. Reushle, A. Antonio, & M. Keppell (Eds.), Open Learning and Formal Credentialing in Higher Education: Curriculum Models and Institutional Policies (pp. 205–222). Hershey, PA: IGI Global. doi:10.4018/978-1-4666-8856-8.ch011

Stevenson, C. N. (2016). Communicating across the Generations: Implications for Higher Education Leadership. In A. Normore, L. Long, & M. Javidi (Eds.), Handbook of Research on Effective Communication, Leadership, and Conflict Resolution (pp. 494–514). Hershey, PA: IGI Global. doi:10.4018/978-1-4666-9970-0.ch026

Swami, B. N., Gobona, T., & Tsimako, J. J. (2017). Academic Leadership: A Case Study of the University of Botswana. In N. Baporikar (Ed.), Innovation and Shifting Perspectives in Management Education (pp. 1–32). Hershey, PA: IGI Global. doi:10.4018/978-1-5225-1019-2.ch001

Timmerman, L. C., & Mulvihill, T. M. (2017). Department Chair Perspectives About Contingent Faculty in Higher Education: Leadership Theory. In S. Mukerji & P. Tripathi (Eds.), Handbook of Research on Administration, Policy, and Leadership in Higher Education (pp. 440–460). Hershey, PA: IGI Global. doi:10.4018/978-1-5225-0672-0.ch017

Tomos, F., Clark, A., Thurariaj, S., Balan, O. C., & Turner, D. (2016). The Emergence of Women Entrepreneurs and Communities of Practice within the Global Context. In S. Buckley, G. Majewski, & A. Giannakopoulos (Eds.), Organizational Knowledge Facilitation through Communities of Practice in Emerging Markets (pp. 85–113). Hershey, PA: IGI Global. doi:10.4018/978-1-5225-0013-1.ch005

Torok, R. (2016). The Role of Women from a Social Media Jihad Perspective: Wife or Warrior? In R. English & R. Johns (Eds.), Gender Considerations in Online Consumption Behavior and Internet Use (pp. 161–184). Hershey, PA: IGI Global. doi:10.4018/978-1-5225-0010-0.ch011

Toulassi, B. (2017). Educational Administration and Leadership in Francophone Africa: 5 Dynamics to Change Education. In S. Mukerji & P. Tripathi (Eds.), Handbook of Research on Administration, Policy, and Leadership in Higher Education (pp. 20–45). Hershey, PA: IGI Global. doi:10.4018/978-1-5225-0672-0.ch002

Tran, B. (2015). The Next Generation of Leaders: Women in Global Leaderships in Hotel Management Industry. In J. Feng, S. Stocklin, & W. Wang (Eds.), Educational Strategies for the Next Generation Leaders in Hotel Management (pp. 16–42). Hershey, PA: IGI Global. doi:10.4018/978-1-4666-8565-9.ch002

Tran, B. (2016). Culturally Gendered: The Institutionalization of Men and Masculinities in Society and Corporations. In N. Mahtab, S. Parker, F. Kabir, T. Haque, A. Sabur, & A. Sowad (Eds.), Discourse Analysis as a Tool for Understanding Gender Identity, Representation, and Equality (pp. 99–135). Hershey, PA: IGI Global. doi:10.4018/978-1-5225-0225-8.ch006

Tran, B. (2016). Gendered Social-Networking Organizations: A View of the Sexed Mentorship Relationships. *International Journal of Organizational and Collective Intelligence*, *6*(2), 26–49. doi:10.4018/IJOCI.2016040103

Van Den Hoven, M., & Litz, D. R. (2016). Organizational Metaphors and the Evaluation of Higher Education Programs, Management Practices, and Change Processes: A UAE Case Study. In E. Espinosa (Ed.), Systemic Knowledge-Based Assessment of Higher Education Programs (pp. 43–68). Hershey, PA: IGI Global. doi:10.4018/978-1-5225-0457-3.ch004

Van Ryneveld, L. (2016). Introducing Educational Technology into the Higher Education Environment: A Professional Development Framework. In K. Dikilitaş (Ed.), Innovative Professional Development Methods and Strategies for STEM Education (pp. 126–136). Hershey, PA: IGI Global. doi:10.4018/978-1-4666-9471-2.ch008

Vargas-Hernández, J. G., & Ibarra, S. T. (2017). Evaluating Higher Education Institutions through Agency and Resource-Capabilities Theories: A Model for Measuring the Perceived Quality of Service. In N. Baporikar (Ed.), Innovation and Shifting Perspectives in Management Education (pp. 246–268). Hershey, PA: IGI Global. doi:10.4018/978-1-5225-1019-2.ch011

Whitehurst, J., & Vander Putten, J. (2014). Communication between Higher Education and Social Networking Sites. In C. Stevenson & J. Bauer (Eds.), Building Online Communities in Higher Education Institutions: Creating Collaborative Experience (pp. 1–22). Hershey, PA: IGI Global. doi:10.4018/978-1-4666-5178-4.ch001

Wittmer, J. L., & Rudolph, C. W. (2015). The Impact of Diversity on Career Transitions over the Life Course. In C. Hughes (Ed.), Impact of Diversity on Organization and Career Development (pp. 151–185). Hershey, PA: IGI Global. doi:10.4018/978-1-4666-7324-3.ch007

Wittmer, J. L., Werth, P. M., & Rudolph, C. W. (2016). Career Transitions and Trajectories for a Diverse Workforce: A Special Focus on Women and Older Workers. In J. Prescott (Ed.), Handbook of Research on Race, Gender, and the Fight for Equality (pp. 492–538). Hershey, PA: IGI Global. doi:10.4018/978-1-5225-0047-6.ch022

Wynne, C. W. (2016). Cultivating Leaders from Within: Transforming Workers into Leaders. In Professional Development and Workplace Learning: Concepts, Methodologies, Tools, and Applications (pp. 1675–1691). Hershey, PA: IGI Global. doi:10.4018/978-1-4666-8632-8.ch091

Xerri, D. (2014). Teachers' Use of Social Networking Sites for Continuing Professional Development. In G. Mallia (Ed.), The Social Classroom: Integrating Social Network Use in Education (pp. 441–464). Hershey, PA: IGI Global. doi:10.4018/978-1-4666-4904-0.ch022

Yuce, S. T., Agarwal, N., Wigand, R. T., Lim, M., & Robinson, R. S. (2014). Bridging Women Rights Networks: Analyzing Interconnected Online Collective Actions. *Journal of Global Information Management*, *22*(4), 1–20. doi:10.4018/jgim.2014100101

Zgheib, P. W. (2015). Sexual Harassment Laws and Their Impact on the Work Environment. In Business Ethics and Diversity in the Modern Workplace (pp. 41–65). Hershey, PA: IGI Global. doi:10.4018/978-1-4666-7254-3.ch004

Zhou, C. (2017). Fostering Creative Problem Solvers in Higher Education: A Response to Complexity of Societies. In C. Zhou (Ed.), Handbook of Research on Creative Problem-Solving Skill Development in Higher Education (pp. 1–23). Hershey, PA: IGI Global. doi:10.4018/978-1-5225-0643-0.ch001

Zhou, C. (2017). Going Towards Adaption, Integration, and Co-Creation: A Conclusion to Developing Creative Problem Solving Skills in Higher Education. In C. Zhou (Ed.), Handbook of Research on Creative Problem-Solving Skill Development in Higher Education (pp. 533–540). Hershey, PA: IGI Global. doi:10.4018/978-1-5225-0643-0.ch024

Zhou, M. Y. (2015). Gender and Education: Equity and Equality in Post Mao China. In M. Zhou (Ed.), Supporting Multiculturalism and Gender Diversity in University Settings (pp. 56–73). Hershey, PA: IGI Global. doi:10.4018/978-1-4666-8321-1.ch004

Compilation of References

Abbott, S. (2014). Hidden curriculum. *The glossary of education reform.* Retrieved from http://edglossary.org/hidden-curriculum

ACT. (2012). Preparing community college students for jobs and careers. Washington, D.C. Retrieved from http://act.rg/research/policymakers/pdf/changing_lives.pdf

ACT. (2016). Job profiling. Washington, D.C. Retrieved from http://www.act.org/content/act/en/products-and-services/workforce-solutions/act-workkeys/job-profiling.html

Alberts, B., Kirschner, M. W., Tilghman, S., & Varmus, H. (2014). Rescuing US biomedical research from its systemic flaws. *Proceedings of the National Academies of Science., 111*(14), 5773–5777. doi:10.1073/pnas.1404402111 PMID:24733905

Alberts, B., Kirschner, M. W., Tilghman, S., & Varmus, H. (2015). Addressing systemic problems in the biomedical research enterprise. *Proceedings of the National Academies of Science., 112*(7), 1912–1913. doi:10.1073/pnas.1500969112 PMID:25691698

Allingham, M. (2002). *Choice Theory.* New York, NY: Oxford University Press. doi:10.1093/actrade/9780192803030.001.0001

American Association of Community Colleges and National Center on Education and the Economy. (2009). *Sustaining Partnerships for Regional Economic Growth.*

American Association of Community Colleges. (2013). *Community colleges past to present.* Retrieved from http://www.aacc.nche.edu/AboutCC/history/Pages/pasttopresent.aspx

Baber, A. (2011). Using community colleges to build a STEM-skilled workforce. *NGA Center for Best Practices.* Retrieved from http://www.nga.org/cms/home/nga-center-for-best-practices/center-publications/page-edu-publications/col2-content/main-content-list/using-community-colleges-to-buil.html

Barbee, J. R. (2005). Advisory technical skills committee. Retrieved from http://files.eric.ed.gov/fulltext/ED521978.pdf

Beach, A., Henderson, C., & Finkelstein, N. (2011). Facilitating change in undergraduate STEM instructional practices: An analytic review of the literature. *Journal of Research in Science Teaching*, *48*(8), 952–984. doi:10.1002/tea.20439

Benigni, V., Ferguson, D., & McGee, B. (2011). Establishing a "renown-gown" relationship: The role of advisory boards in communication programs. Retrieved from http://web.b.ebscohost.com.lib-e2.lib.ttu.edu/ehost/pdfviewer/pdfviewer?sid=8d8ede9c-90be-48fd-9764-5d0d90b803c1%40sessionmgr111&vid=23&hid=123

Bess, J. L., & Dee, J. R. (2008). *Understanding college and university organizations: Theories for effective policy and practice* (Vol. II). City, VA: Stylus.

Beyer, B. K. (1995). Critical thinking and problem-solving. Retrieved from http://www.utc.edu/walker-center-teaching-learning/teaching-resources/ct-ps.php

Blum, J. (2016, December 24). Oil rig jobs might soon fall to technology. *Midland Reporter Telegram, pp. 1A, 6A.*

Bray, J. (2011, January 17). Career and technical colleges can help retrain the unemployed. *The Chronicle of Higher Education.* Retrieved from http://chronicle.com/article/CareerTechnical-Colleges/125977/

Brown, R. A., & Shen, H. (2017). Challenges and solutions of higher education in the Eastern Caribbean States. Retrieved from https://eric.ed.gov/?q=higher+education+networking&ft=on&id=EJ1126023

Burke, L., & Miller, M. (1999). Taking the mystery out of intuitive decision-making. Retrieved from http://aspnet.cob.ohio.edu/mc/pmba_co_3/Class/CMBA602Strategic/TheMaterialReadings/Module%202%20Readings/R%234%20Taking%20the%20Mystery%20out%20of%20Intuitive%20Decision%20Making.pdf

Business and Higher Education Forum. (2013). Forging Strategic Business Partnerships to Develop the 21st Century Workforce: A Case Study of the University of Houston's Undergraduate Petroleum Engineering Program. Retrieved from https://eric.ed.gov/?q=+biomedical+workforce+advisory +committees&ft=on&ff1=dtySince_2013&id=ED559641/

Caparosa, C. (1984). Advisory Committees. Clute Institute. Retrieved from https://www.cluteinstitute.com/ojs/index.php/CIER/article/download/8308/8338

Carlson, P., Holm, R., & Uvalde, R. (2011). Building regional partnerships for economic growth and opportunity. *Jobs for the Future.* Retrieved from http://futureworks-web.com/pdfs/Building_Regional_Partnerships.pdf

Carson, (2011). A meta-analysis of different forms of shared leadership-team performance relations. Retrieved from http://jom.sagepub.com/content/early/2014/03/06/0149206314525205

Chakma, J., Sun, G. H., Steinberg, J. D., Sammut, S. M., & Jagsi, R. (2014). Asias Ascent – Global trends in biomedical R&D expenditures. *The New England Journal of Medicine*, *370*(1), 3–6. doi:10.1056/NEJMp1311068 PMID:24382062

Cohen, A., & Brawer, F. (2008). *The American community college*. San Francisco, CA: Jossey-Bass, Inc.

Collin College. (2011). Advisory committee handbook. Retrieved from http://www.cc.edu/handbook/advisory.html

Collin Community College. (2016). *Advisory committee handbook*. Retrieved from http://www.cc.edu/handbook/advisory/html

Committee on Biomedical Scientific Workforce (CBSW), Johns Hopkins University, Office of the Provost. (n. d.). Initiatives. Retrieved from http://web.jhu.edu/administration/provost/initiatives/Committee on_the_Biomedical_Scientific_Workforce/index.html

Committee on Comparative National Innovation Policies. Best practice for the 21st century, National Research Council (CCNIP). (2012). Rising to the Challenge: U.S. Innovation Policy for the Global Economy. National Academies Press. Washington, D.C.

Committee on Research Universities, National Research Council. (CRUNRC). (2012) Research Universities and the Future of America: Ten Breakthrough Actions Vital to Our Nation's Prosperity and Security. National Academies Press. Washington D.C.

Conte, M. L. (2017). Globalization and changing trends of biomedical research output. *Journal of Clinical Investigation Insight*.

Council of Graduate Schools. (2017). Issue Brief: Tax Reform – Education Related Provisions. Retrieved from http://cgsnet.org/sites/default/files/Tax_reform_ISSUE_BRIEF_May_2017.pdf

Council of Graduate Schools. (2017). Updated: CGS Statement Regarding Administration's Executive Order on Immigration. Retrieved from http://cgsnet.org/updated-cgs-statement-regarding-administration%E2%80%99s-executive-order-immigration

Cronen, S., & Murphy, C. (2013) Participation in noncredit and occupational training and education. American Institute for Research. Retrieved from https://nces.ed.gov/surveys/gemena/pdf/NoncreditPaper_AIR_Final508.pdf

Daniels, R. J. (2015). A generation at risk: Young investigators and the future of biomedical workforce. *Proceedings of the National Academies of Science.*, *112*(2), 313–318. doi:10.1073/pnas.1418761112 PMID:25561560

Davis, J. L., & Davis, H. (2009). The learning Organization implemented in education through advisory committees. Retrieved from http://web.b.ebscohost.com.lib-e2.lib.ttu.edu/ehost/pdfviewer/pdfviewer?vid=4&sid=8d8ede9c-90be-48fd-9764-5d0d90b803c1%40sessionmgr111&hid=123

Day, M. (2001). Faculty perceptions of advisory committee effectiveness at two-year technical college. *Journal of Education for Business*, *110*(2), 194–198.

DeMatthews, D., Mungal, A., & Carrola, P. (2015, Winter). Despite best intentions: A critical analysis of social justice leadership and decision making. *Administrative Issues Journal.*, *5*(2), 17–37. doi:10.5929/ 2015.5.2.4

Deming, E. (1986). *Out of the Crisis*. Cambridge, MA: MIT Press.

Deming, W. E. (1994). *The New Economics for Industry, Government and Education*. Cambridge: MAMIT Press.

Destefano, D. (2011). Khalifa Bin Zayed Al Nahyan Foundation Provides MD Anderson with $150 Million Grant Retrieved from https://www.mdanderson.org/publications/conquest/fall-2011/khalifa-bin-zayed-al-nahyan-foundation.html

DiMattina, C. (n. d.). Lessons in collaboration: Principles in the governance of an industry advisory board. Retrieved from https://www.acteonline.org/uploadedFiles/Assets_and_Documents/Global/files/Publications/RPB_IndustryAdvisoryBoards.pdf

Dixon, H. (1990). *Communication*. Houston, TX: Washington and Lee University.

Dougherty, K. J., & Townsend, B. K. (2006). Community college missions: A theoretical and historical perspective. New Direction for Community Colleges, (136), 5-13.

European Commission. (2007). Communications from the Commission: Improving knowledge transfer between research institutions and industry across Europe. Retrieved from http://ec.europa.eu/invest-in-research/pdf/download_en/knowledge_transfe_07.pdf

Fauci, A. S. (1998). New and reemerging diseases: The Importance of Biomedical Research. *Emerging Infectious Diseases*, *4*(3), 374–378. doi:10.3201/eid0403.980308 PMID:9716949

FCA. (2017). Advisory Committee. Retrieved from http://www.finishingcontractors.org/members-resources/advisory-committees

Federation of American Societies for Experimental Biology. (2015). *Sustaining discovery in biomedical and medical sciences: A framework for discussion*. Bethesda, MD, USA: FASEB.

Finegold, D. (2005). Alternative Career options in the biomedical industry: The professional science master's degree. *Nature Biotechnology*, *23*(4), 503–504. doi:10.1038/nbt0405-503 PMID:15815680

Follett, M. P. (1918). *Group Organization*. New York, NY: Longmans, Green and Company.

Freedman, T. (2009). *Career Opportunities in Biotechnology and Drug Development* (1st ed.). Cold Spring Harbor Laboratory Press.

Gerbi, S. A., Garrison, H. H., & Perkins, J. P. (2001). Education. Workforce alternatives to graduate students? *Science*, *292*(5521), 1489–1490. doi:10.1126/science.1059268 PMID:11379627

GIPWE. (2010, 2015). Guidelines for instructional workforce education. Texas Higher Education Coordinating Board.

GIPWE. (2015). Guidelines for instructional workforce education. Texas Higher Education Coordinating Board.

Gonzalez-Rivera, C. (2016). Building the workforce of the future. *Center for an urban future.* Retrieved from http://files.eric.ed.gov/fulltext/ED567868.pdf

Greenstone, M., & Looney, A. (2011). *Building America's job skills with effective workforce programs: A training strategy to raise wages and increase work opportunities.* The Hamilton Project. Retrieved from http://www.brookings.edu/~/media/research/files/papers/2011/11/training%20greenstone%20looney/11_training_greenstone_looney.pdf

Greenwald, T. (2017). How AI is transforming the workforce. *Workplace Technology. The Wall Street Journal. 13 March 2017.R1.*

Grigsby R.K. (2006). Are you really a team player? *Academic Physician and Scientist.* 4-5.

Grigsby, R. K. (2008). *Committee, Task Force, Team: What's the difference? Why Does It Matter?* (pp. 4–5). Academic Physician and Scientist.

Guidelines for Instructional Programs in Workforce Education. (2015). Guidelines for instructional workforce education. Texas Higher Education Coordinating Board.

Hamilton, V. (2004). *Building communities with a competitive workforce advantage. Sustaining Partnerships for Regional Economic Growth* (pp. 30–34). Washington, D.C.: American Association of Community Colleges.

Haralson, L. (2010). What is workforce development? *Federal Reserve Bank of St. Lewis.* Retrieved from https://www.stlouisfed.org/Publications/Bridges/Spring-2010/What-is-Workforce-Development#fn1

Harrison, W. G. (1975). The advisory committee in the community college: An overview. Retrieved from www.ehis.ebscohost.com.lib-e2.lib.ttu.edu

Hashish, E. A., Hamouda, G. M., & Taha, E. (2015). Nursing students' perception of conflict management styles of their nursing educators. Retrieved from https://eric.ed.gov/?q=conflict+management+with+committees&id=EJ1079105

Heffernan, M. (2015). Making effective decisions. PMI's Pulse of the Profession. Retrieved from https://www.pmi.org/learning/thought-leadership/pulse/capturing-the-value-of-project-management

Heitman, E. (2005). Ivey Tech forms new workforce development department. *Community College Week*, *18*(6), 17.

Hodges, R. (2012). *The road half traveled.* East Lansing, MI: Michigan State University Press.

Holzer, H. J. (2008). Workforce training: What works? Who benefits? Retrieved from http://www.familyimpactseminars.org/s_wifis28c02.pdf

Holzer, H. J. (2010). Connecting people to work. Retrieved from https://www.brookings.edu/wp-content/uploads/2016/06/polarization_jobs_policy_holzer.pdf

Hughes, B. (2016). Worldwide Contributions. Retrieved from https://www.bakerhughes.com / company/corporate-social-responsibility/people-and-society/community-engagement/worldwide-contributions

Jacobs, R. (2007). Emergence of Workforce Development. *Economicmodeling*. Retrieved from www.economicmodeling.com/resources/wp-content/uploads/2007/11/jacobs_hawley-emergenceofworkforcedevelopment.pdf

Johnson, L. (2013). Bridging the gap between education and workforce. Retrieved from http://www.ascd.org/publications/newsletters/policy-priorities/vol20/num03/Career-Readines

Johnson, N., Oliff, P., & Williams, E. (2011). An update on state budget cuts. Retrieved from http://www.mobilelottery.com/wp-content/uploads/2010/05/Update-On-State-Budget-Cuts.pdf

Jones, G. (2006). *Organizational theory design and change* (5th ed.). Saddle River, NJ: Prentice Hall.

Kay, S. (2015). Africa's leadership in biomedical research: Shifting the center of gravity. *Science Translational Medicine*, *7*(314), 1–3. doi:10.1126/scitranslmed.aad5529 PMID:26582894

Kazis, R. (2011). *Brookings-Rockefeller Project on state metropolitan innovation.* Washington, D.C.: Jobs for the Future.

Kerka, S. (2002). *Effective advisory committees.* (ERIC Information Analyses ED463411). Retrieved from ehis.ebscohost.com.lib-e2.lib.ttu.edu

Kilcrease, K. M. (2011). Faculty perceptions of business advisory boards: The challenge for effective communication. *Journal of Education for Business*, *86*(2), 78–83. doi:10.1080/08832323.2010.480989

Kokkonen, L., & Almonkari, M. (2015). Teaching networking: An interpersonal communication competence perspective. Received from https://eric.ed.gov/?q=higher+education+networking&ft=on&id=ED565025

Kolata, G. (2016) Lost in Academia: So Many Research Scientists, So Few Openings as Professors. *New York Times*. Retrieved from https://www.nytimes.com/2016/07/14/upshot/so-many-research-scientists-so-few-openings-as-professors.html

Korn, M. (19 December 2016). *College enrollment slumps.* Wall Street Journal. p. A3.

Kress, A. M. (2012). A community-based approach to growing the middle-sill workforce. Community College Week. Retrieved from http://www.ccwee.com/news/templates/template.aspx?articleid=3015&zoneid=7

Kristiansen, C. (2014) America is losing biomedical research leadership to Asia. *Fogarty International Center.* Retrieved from https://www.fic.nih.gov/News/GlobalHealthMatters/january-february-2014/Pages/spending-investment-biomedical-research-development.aspx

Landro, L. (2017). How to (really) get patients to take more control over their medical decisions. *Wall Street Journal.* 27 February 2017. R1.

Lane Community College. (2013). *CAHM Successful Committee Presentation.* Retrieved from http://www.lanecc.edu/ctecc/advisory-committees

Langley, M. (2015). Making effective decisions. PMI's Pulse of the Profession. Retrieved from https://www.pmi.org/learning/thought-leadership/pulse/capturing-the-value-of-project-management

LaRose, C. (2014). Workforce development in America: A brief history. Retrieved from https://www.linkedin.com/pulse/20141015154244-57121104-workforce-development-in-america-a-brief-history/

Leatherman, C. (1998). Report by governing-boards group urges speedier approaches to making decisions. The Chronicle of Higher Education. Retrieved from http://chronicle.com/article/Report-by-Governing-Boards/104811/

Lewis, M. (2017). *The Undoing Project.* New York, NY: W.W. Norton & Company.

Library of Congress. (2010). Education and the workforce committee. Retrieved from https://www.congress.gov/committee/house-education-and-the-workforce/hsed0

Lovits, B. (2001). *Leaving the Ivory Tower: The Causes and Consequences of Departure from Doctoral Study*. Rowman & Littlefield.

Lu, P. et al., (2016). National and State-Specific Td and Tdap Vaccination of Adult Populations.

Massachusetts Department of Higher Education. (2014). Technology talent initiative workforce plan. *The Vision Project*. Retrieved from http://www.mass.edu/bhe/lib/reports/2014-05-05DHETechnologyWorkforcePlan.pdf

McEwen, M. (2016, December 17). Unemployment falls for 2nd straight month. *Midland Reporter Telegram.*, *1A*, 4A.

McShane, S., & Von Glinow, M. (2014). *Organizational Behavior*. New York, NY: McGraw-Hill Companies, Inc.

Meeder, H. & Pawlowski, B. (2012). Building advisory boards that matter. *Techniques*, *2*(28).

Mele, D. (2006). Follett's organizational approach. Retrieved from http://www.iese.edu/research/pdfs/DI-0618-E

Members of the 2005 "Rising Above the Gathering Storm" Committee. (2010). *Rising Above the Gathering Storm, Revisited: Rapidly Approaching Category 5*. Washington D.C.: National Academies Press.

Metcalf, H., & Urwick, M. (2013). *Dynamic administration: The collected papers of Mary Parker Follett. Mansfield Centre*. CT: Martino Publishing.

Mintz, C. S. (2010). Non-traditional Career Options for Life Scientists. *ASBMB today*. Retrieved from http://www.asbmb.org/asbmbtoday/asbmbtoday_article.aspx?id=7868

Mintzberg, H. (1979). *The structuring of organizations*. Upper Saddle River, NJ: Prentice Hall.

National Center for Education and the Economy. (2009). Community college advisory panel. Retrieved from https://professionals.collegeboard.org/higher-ed/community-colleges/advisory-panel

National Center for Education Statistics. (2010). *Career/Technical Education (CTE) Statistics*. (Table P108). Retrieved from http://nces.ed.gov/surveys/ctes/tables/P108.asp

National Center for Education Statistics. (2012). *Higher education: Gaps in access and persistence study*. Retrieved from http://nces.ed.gov/pubs2012/2012046/index.asp

National Center for Education Statistics. (2012). U.S. Background Information Prepared for the OECD Postsecondary Vocational Education and Training "Skills Beyond School" Study. Retrieved from http://nces.ed.gov/surveys/ctes/pdf/Postsec VET.pdf

National Council for Excellence in Critical Thinking. (1987). Defining critical thinking. Retrieved from http://www.criticalthinking.org/pages/defining-critical-thinking/766

Northouse, P. G. (2013). *Leadership: Theory and practice*. Los Angeles, CA: Sage Publishing.

Oliff, P., Palacios, V., Johnson, I., & Leachman, M. (2013). Recent deep state higher education cuts may harm students and the economy for years to come. Retrieved from http://www.cbpp.org/files/3-19-13sfp.pdf

Paul, R. W. (1995). Critical thinking. Retrieved from http://isites.harvard.edu/fs/docs/icb.topic265890.files/Critical_Thinking_File/06_CT_Exten

Pelletier, S. G. (2012). High-performing committees: What makes them work? Retrieved from https://www.agb.org/trusteeship/2012/5/high-performing-committees-what-makes-them-work

Perna, L. (2012). *Preparing today's students for tomorrow's jobs in metropolitan America*. Philadelphia, PA: University of Pennsylvania Press.

Pettigrew, A. M. (2014). *The politics of organizational decision-making*. New York, NY: Routledge.

Pramesh, C. S., Venkataramanan, R., Suvarna, V., Goel, N. S., Lakshman, S., Venkatesh, V., & Badwe, R. et al. (2016). Involvement of general public in biomedical research. *Perspectives in Clinical Research.*, *7*(4), 152–155. doi:10.4103/2229-3485.192029 PMID:27843788

Prevention and Control of Influenza with Vaccines (PCIV): Recommendations of the advisory committee on immunizations practices, United States. (2015-2016). Influenza Season. *American Journal of Transplantation*, 15(10), 2767–2775. doi:10.1111/ajt.13505 PMID:26382204

Price, D. V., & Roberts, B. (2009). Improving student success by strengthening developmental education in community colleges: The role of state policy. The Working Poor Families Project. Retrieved from http://www.workingpoorfamilies.org/pdfs/WPFP_policybrief_winter08-09.pdf

Rahim, M. A. (2011). Managing conflict in organizations. Retrieved from http://enactskills.eu/wordpress /en/learning-materials/interpersonal-conflict/

Riendeau, A. J. (1967). *The role of the advisory committee in occupational education in the junior college*. Retrieved from ehis.ebscohost.com.lib-e2.lib.ttu.edu

Rodgers, B. D. (2013). When is education a disservice? *The FASEB Journal*, *27*(12), 4678–4681. doi:10.1096/fj.13-235762 PMID:23975933

Schaeffer, D., & Rouse, D. (2014). Effective academic advisory committee relationships. *Contemporary issues in education research*. Retrieved from http://files.eric.ed.gov/fulltext/EJ1073283.pdf

Scientific Management Review Board (SMRB). (2014). Draft Report on approaches to assess the Value of Biomedical Research Supported by NIH. Retrieved from: https://smrb.od.nih.gov/documents/reports/VOBR%20SMRB__Report_2014.pdf

Sena, M., Sena, J. A., & Crable, E. A. (2010). Faculty perceptions on the goals and achievements of information executive board information. Retrieved from http://isedj.org/8/41/ISEDJ.8(41).Sena.pdf

Smith, P. (2013). *Creative Experience: Mary Parker Follett*. Mansfield Center, CT: Martino Publishing.

Soares, L. (2010). The power of the education-industry partnership. Retrieved from http://americanprogress.org/issues/labor/report/2010/10/04/8518/thepoweroftheeducation

Soares, L. *The power of the education-industry partnership*. Retrieved from http://americanprogress.org/issues/labor/report/2010/10/04/8518/thepoweroftheeducation

Spector, B. (2012). *Implementing organizational change: Theory into practice* (3rd ed.). Saddle River, NJ: Prentice Hall.

Steinbrook, R. (2004). Science, Politics and Federal Advisory Committees. *The New England Journal of Medicine*, *350*(14), 1454–1460. doi:10.1056/NEJMhpr033416 PMID:15070798

Stevens, L. (2016). Amazon gets on jobs bandwagon. *The Wall Street Journal*, January 13. B1/B4.

Teitel, L. (1994). *The advisory committee advantage: Creating an effective strategy for programmatic improvement*. Washington, D.C.: The George Washington University.

Tesluk, P. E., & Marrone, J. A. (2011). Shared leadership in teams. Retrieved from http://amj.aom .org/content/50/5/1217.abstract

Texas Higher Education Coordinating Board. (2014). *Advisory Boards*. Retrieved from http://www.thecb.state.tx.us/index.cfm?objectid=8C1EF7E7-A71E-47E6-53FE5EFA82F3880C

Texas State Library. (2016). Texas historical records advisory board. Retrieved from https://www.tsl.texas.gov/thrab

Texas Workforce Commission. (2013). Community & Workforce Partners. Retrieved from http://www.twc.state.tx.us/customers/cwp/community-workforce-partners.html

The Research Universities Futures Consortium. (2012). *The Current Health and Future Well-Being of the American Research University*. Philadelphia, PA: Elsevier.

The University of Mississippi. (2017). Advisory Committees. Retrieved from https://www2.umc.edu/Administration/Centers_and_Institutes/Mississippi_Center_for_Clinical_and_Translational_Research/External_Advisory_Committee.aspx

Tonn, J. (2003). *Mary P. Follett: Creating democracy, transforming management*. New Haven, CT: Yale Publishing. doi:10.12987/yale/9780300096217.001.0001

US Department of Labor. (2016). Advisory committee on increasing competitive integrated employment for individuals with disabilities. Retrieved from https://www.dol.gov/odep/topics/wioa.htm

US Department of Labor. (2016). *The employment situation*. Retrieved from https://www.bls.gov/news.release/pdf/empsit.pd

Viergever, R. F., & Hendriks, T. C. C. (2016). The 10 largest public and philanthropic funders of health research in the world: What they fund and how they distribute their funds. *Health Research Policy and Systems*, *14*(1), 12. doi:10.1186/s12961-015-0074-z PMID:26892771

Vocational Education Act, 1963. Public Law 88-210o Part A. Retrieved from http://cte.unt.edu/about/cte-history-of-legislation

Wethe, D. (2017). Drilling is back. What about the workers? *Bloomberg Businessweek.*, *30*(January), 14–15.

Workforce Development Overview. (2012). Employment & career development. *Employment Security Department.* Retrieved from http://www.wa.gov/esd/training/elearning/business/01-01.pdf

Working Group on the Diversity in the Biomedical Research Workforce (WGDBRW) and The Advisory Committee to the Director. (2012). Draft Report of the Advisory Committee to the Director Working Group on Diversity in the Biomedical Research Workforce. Retrieved from https://acd.od.nih.gov/documents/reports/DiversityBiomedicalResearchWorkforceReport.pdf

World Economic Forum. (2016). Future workforce strategies. Retrieved from http://reports.weforum.org/future-of-jobs-2016/future-workforce-strategy/http://reports.weforum.org/future-of-jobs-2016/future-workforce-strategy/

About the Contributors

Argentina Ornelas, Ph.D., received her doctorate in Chemistry from Texas A&M University. She has training in basic science research in biology and chemistry. After graduate training, she pursued a postdoctoral training position at MD Anderson Cancer Center, where she was an NCI R25T Cancer Prevention Research Training Fellow in the Cancer Prevention Research Training Program, and the department of Cancer Systems Imaging. It was at MD Anderson that she discovered the importance of the engagement of advisory committees in the successful development of biomedical research training and education. As an active participant of the postdoctoral association at MD Anderson, she firsthand observed the value of advisory committees in the training component of biomedical research education, in order to advance the scientific and health enterprise, as well as to specifically improve the professional training experience of research fellows, all of which can result in ample improvements in the biomedical research workforce.

Julie Neal, Ed.D., earned her doctorate in Higher Education from Texas Tech University; MA in Humanities-Literature from California State University, DH; and BA in Political Science and English from the University of Texas, PB. She has 20 years of educational experience with private, public, and community-college levels in the areas of English, speech, humanities, literature, math, history, geography, and ITV dual credit. Also, included in her years of teaching experience include Teacher of the Year at two public institutions, teaching the deaf at SWCID in Big Spring, Texas and teaching students with special needs in Midland, Texas. Her administrative experience includes Dean of Lamesa Campus for Howard College. Dr. Neal's committee experience involves Core, Critical Thinking Team, Strategic Planning, Program Reviews, SACS Team, Instructional and Workforce Education, Vison, Council, Online Planning, STEM, READe, eLearning, Rotary, Admissions, Advisory, and Affirmative Action committees.

Index

O

P

R

S

V

W

www.ingramcontent.com/pod-product-compliance
Lightning Source LLC
LaVergne TN
LVHW062125200926
848484LV00007B/1765